ON THE JUDGMENT OF HISTORY

RUTH BENEDICT BOOK SERIES

RUTH BENEDICT BOOK SERIES

Edited by David Scott and Elizabeth A. Povinelli

With Series Committee Members Nadia Abu El-Haj, Vanessa Agard-Jones,
Zoe Crossland, Maria José de Abreu, and Naor Ben-Yehoyada

Named after one of the founders of American anthropology and the Columbia
Department of Anthropology, the Ruth Benedict Book Series is inspired by
Benedict's passionate engagement with the critical political, aesthetic, and theoretical problems of the twentieth century but places them in the global conditions of the twenty-first. Contributions to the series explore contemporary
critical thought in politics and aesthetics through a deep knowledge of the global
condition in specific localities and regions. The scope of the series is capaciously
theoretical and determinately international with special emphasis on settler-
colonial, postcolonial, and capitalist regimes. The books present crisp interventions in a multiplicity of disciplines, but are also statements whose reckoning
cuts across the critical humanistic and social sciences.

ON THE
JUDGMENT OF
HISTORY

JOAN WALLACH SCOTT

COLUMBIA UNIVERSITY PRESS   *New York*

COLUMBIA UNIVERSITY PRESS
Publishers Since 1893
New York   Chichester, West Sussex
cup.columbia.edu

Library of Congress Cataloging-in-Publication Data
Names: Scott, Joan Wallach, author. | Scott, Joan Wallach.
In the name of history.
Title: On the judgment of history / Joan Wallach Scott.
Description: New York : Columbia University Press, 2020. | Series: Ruth
Benedict book series | See also: In the name of history by Joan Wallach Scott.
| Includes bibliographical references and index.
Identifiers: LCCN 2020004401 (print) | LCCN 2020004402 (ebook) |
ISBN 9780231196949 (cloth) | ISBN 9780231196956 (paperback) |
ISBN 9780231551908 (ebook)
Subjects: LCSH: History—Philosophy. | Historiography. | Nationalism—
History. | Racism—History. | Nuremberg Trial of Major German War
Criminals, Nuremberg, Germany, 1945–1946—History. | South Africa.
Truth and Reconciliation Commission—History. | Reparations for
historical injustices—United States—History.
Classification: LCC D16.9 .S427 2020 (print) | LCC D16.9 (ebook) |
DDC 901—dc23
LC record available at https://lccn.loc.gov/2020004401
LC ebook record available at https://lccn.loc.gov/2020004402

Cover design: Chang Jae Lee

But whatever this new understanding of the past holds to be irrelevant—shards created by the selection of materials, remainders left aside by an explication—comes back, despite everything, on the edge of discourse or in its rifts and crannies; "resistances," "survivals," or delays discretely perturb the pretty order of a line of "progress" or a system of interpretation.

—Michel de Certeau, *The Writing of History*

CONTENTS

PREFACE

History, Race, Nation

> The current amazement that the things we are experiencing
> are "still" possible in the twentieth century is not philosophical.
> This amazement is not the beginning of knowledge—unless it is
> the knowledge that the view of history which gives rise to it is
> untenable.
>
> —Walter Benjamin, *Theses on the Philosophy of History*, XIII

I began to think about the notion of the judgment of history
in 2017 during the Charlottesville riots, when Confederate
flags flew and swastikas appeared in large numbers and then
when heil Hitler salutes welcomed white supremacist Richard
Spencer's inflammatory orations on campuses across the country. Hadn't the Nazis been declared losers of World War II,
and morally out of bounds? Wasn't "never again"—the vow of
democratic citizens and leaders alike—the promise of the
Nuremberg (and later Eichmann) trials? What had become of
the idea that the evil of Nazism was banished forever from the
political stage? Listening to the chants of the torch-bearing Ku
Klux Klan reenactors, I thought: Didn't the Civil War end slavery not only as a practice, but as an acceptable idea? Hadn't the
civil rights movement made racial equality a national aspira-
tion, if not a reality? Then how to explain then Attorney General Jeff Sessions's evident preference for segregation or the
Senate candidate and white supremacist Roy Moore's comment
that the last time America was great was during slavery? The
lack of any shame at the public avowal of these ideas suggests

not just defiance, but refusal of what was supposed to have been history's judgment.

This became more apparent to me while following the Mueller hearings in the summer of 2019. Special Counsel Robert Mueller's report on Russian interference in the 2016 election and the Trump administration's collusion with it was, in effect, a judgment of history—or at least it was anticipated to be one. Many had looked to Mueller as a savior: he would expose the crimes of the Trump administration, correct the record of lies we had been enduring, and bring justice to the land. Instead, as soon as the report was issued, its contents were misrepresented by Attorney General William Barr. Misrepresented is the wrong word, flatly denied is better; Barr offered a conclusion that the report, which stated clearly that it could *not* exonerate the president of the charge of obstruction of justice, had declared him innocent of that crime. Worse, few Americans read the hundreds of pages of the report, members of Congress included. Its careful delineation of issues, and its indictment and conviction of Trump associates for any number of illegal activities, did not reverse the disastrous course of things; it surely did not convince most Republican legislators of the dangerous path they had chosen to follow. They spent their time during the hearings attacking the veracity and objectivity of the report and its author, even as they rarely disputed the conclusions it had reached. Their craven submission to Trump, their willingness to condone crime in the interests of political ambition, was horrifying to behold. As I lamented this situation to a friend, she sought to console me by pointing out that, if nothing else, these corrupters of democracy would be condemned by the "judgment of history."

As a historian, I know that there is no closure for history, no single story that can be told. I am aware of the number of histories being written that challenge the validity and coherence of the master narratives with which we have been schooled. Still, I think like my friend, I naively (reflexively?) held to the popular belief that there is a certain moral impeccability about history's judgment. It is a secular version of the biblical day of reckoning at the End of Times, serving the same phantasmatic function, providing transcendent reassurance for one's moral positions. We often use the words "the judgment of history," or we suggest that we need to be "on the right side of history," projecting onto "history" confirmation of our wishes for the future. Fidel Castro, standing before the court that would send him to prison in 1953, challenged the judges to "Condemn me. It does not matter. History will absolve me."[1] Telford Taylor, an assistant prosecutor at the Nuremberg Trials, writing a critique of the Vietnam War many years later, noted that "it may be unlikely that our leaders will be called upon to answer at the bar of some future international tribunal, but there is also the bar of history."[2] Barack Obama, citing Martin Luther King citing the abolitionist Theodore Parker, was certain that "the arc of the moral universe is long, but it bends toward justice."[3] As I write this there are, almost daily, comments in newspapers and other media that "history will be the judge" of some person or event whose unacceptable behavior seems otherwise immune to punishment. To take some examples, here is the journalist Michael Luo writing in the *New Yorker* about the scandal of Trump's immigration policy: "It is up to Cucinnelli, others in the Trump Administration, and potential enablers in the Republican Party to decide how they wish history to judge them, even as they carry on a shameful legacy that American democracy has struggled to escape."[4] Or, there are the comments of Representative John Lewis on the Democrats' decision to launch an impeachment investigation of Donald Trump. Lewis explained that they were "moved by the spirit of history to take action to protect and preserve the integrity of our nation."[5] Yet another is from the former FBI director James Comey, justifying his decision to make public the investigation of Hillary Clinton's emails: "He predicted that history would judge him kindly for prizing disclosure over concealment."[6] We tend to draw a measure of comfort from the idea that, in the long run, history (History?) is an autonomous moral force that can motivate action and set straight the record of human deeds and misdeeds. A young peasant in hiding from Franco's forces at the end of the Spanish Civil War created a document intended for the "Court of History," where, the anthropologist Susana Narotzky tells us, "the Future is imagined as a place where Truth reigns supreme."[7] Writing in 1934, Max Horkheimer put it this way: "When you are at the lowest ebb, exposed to an eternity of torment inflicted upon you by other human beings, you cherish, as a dream of deliverance, the idea that a being will come who will stand in the light and bring truth and justice for you. You don't even need this to happen in your lifetime, nor in the lifetime of those who are torturing you to death, but one day, whenever it comes, all will nonetheless be repaired. . . . It is bitter to be misunderstood and to die in obscurity. It is to the honour of historical research that it projects light into that obscurity."[8] In these examples, the judgment of history is assumed not only to confirm moral stands taken, but it is also based on the belief that truth will out in the end; history is the final arbiter of that truth.

My friend's echo of these appeals to the judgment of history made me realize how powerful a fantasy the notion is, how strong its messianic promise holds even for skeptical secularists like myself, even in an age when "the end of history" has been declared, and when belief in reassuring progressive master narratives ended sometime in the twentieth century. After all, there is no history (or History), apart from what we make of it; no higher court of judgment than our own moral compass; no way to disentangle moral argument from political purpose. The invocation of history's judgment suggests an external force at work. It is projection in two senses. One psychic: our own wishes attributed outward, in this case to a seemingly extrahuman, necessarily progressive force—History. The other temporal: assessing actions—our own and those of others—from the perspective of an imagined redemptive future that we will have had a hand in creating.

The persistence of references to the judgment of history seemed to me worth thinking about critically: Was it a motive for action or a form of consolation for political impotence? How had the notion of history's judgment functioned in the past? How did its explicit moral message relate to a politics being addressed? Was there a relationship between past, present, and future being presumed that needed interrogation?

Those were the thoughts simmering in my head when I was invited to do the Ruth Benedict Lectures at Columbia University. The occasion seemed a good moment to try to sort them out. Little did I realize not only that when I chose "The Judgment of History" as my topic I would be exploring the survival of an idea of history in popular discourse long after its presumed death, but also that I would be pushed by my colleagues to think about the politics of history in new ways. Having written a great deal about gender and the politics of history, this was a challenge: to think about the relationship between the state, the moral, and the political as it involved uses of the concept of history itself.[9] And to think about it in Benjamin's terms, as requiring a different view of history than the one conventionally brought to bear on this topic.

"World History Is the World's Tribunal"

The moral stance implied in "the judgment of history" draws enduring distinctions between good and evil, justice and injustice,

equality and inequality, right and wrong, truth and falsehood—
as if in her wisdom, Clio will rescue us mortals from the errors
of our ways. As if History were the ultimate demonstration of
the inherent moral goodness of human reason, a reason divorced
from power. We can find this belief articulated by Hegel, who,
writing of the "dialectic of the finite nature of these minds [of
states]," proposed that "out of it arises the universal mind, the
mind of the world, free from all restriction, producing itself as
that which exercises its right—and its right is the highest right
of all—over these finite minds in the 'history of the world which
is the world's court of judgment.' "[10] Hegel was perhaps echoing
Friedrich Schiller, who, in 1784, had declared that "world history is the world's tribunal."[11] Reinhart Koselleck notes that
"Since the French Revolution, history has become a subject fur-
nished with divine epithets of omnipotence, universal justice,
and sanctity."[12]

Koselleck distinguishes the tribunal of history from earlier
Christian forecasts of the Last Judgment—it is a matter of both
a different temporality and a different agency. On the question
of time, apocalyptic prophecy was replaced by more immediate
"rational" prognoses. As a result, the sense of time accelerated
and the experience of change (even in one's lifetime) became
fundamental. In place of the "multitude of individual histories"
that characterized earlier notions, modernity's history was conceived to be unitary and linear, "always constrained by a temporal
sequence."[13] (Walter Benjamin referred to this as "homogeneous empty time.")[14] The agency is at once human and transcendent: humans make history, but History is also conceived as
an autonomous force that is, however, the culmination and
expression of an inevitably progressive, universal human reason.
History is the realization (the projection into the future) of the
best that rational humans can be. Writes Koselleck, "Wherever
the 'makeability' of history might be implied, it was lent redoubled

emphasis as soon as the actor invoked a history which, at the same time, objectively indicated the path he should take."[15] Michel de Certeau puts it this way: "In every history a process of meaning can be found which always aims at fulfilling the meaning of History."[16]

The standard of judgment expected of that History is associated with the Enlightenment belief that there is but one History, which moves in an ever-improving direction: forward, upward, cumulatively positive. Kant's "Idea of a Universal History" talked of the "regular course" of "the play of liberty of the human will." Despite individual variations, he wrote, there was for the whole species "a continually progressive, though slow, unfolding of its predispositions . . . that happen . . . according to constant laws of nature."[17] Progress was the prevailing master narrative from the eighteenth century onward. It was derived from the idea of history as inherent in the very being of human and animal species; evolution was our teleology, reason and civilization were its manifestations. By the nineteenth century, writes Michel Foucault, "History . . . is certainly the most erudite, the most aware, the most conscious, and possibly the most cluttered area of our memory; but it is equally the depths from which all beings emerge into their precarious, glittering existence. Since it is the mode of being of all that is given us in experience, History has become the unavoidable element in our thought."[18] That History—conceived as it was in evolutionary terms—was as much about the future as the past; to this day, it gives rise to what Koselleck calls "a concept of historical hope."[19] There is an unmistakable moral dimension to this notion of history; Koselleck, referring to Kant, says the philosopher offers "history as a temporalized house of correction for morality."[20] If the direction of history is necessarily progressive, then the moral value of our actions must be measured by their contribution to that end.

State and Nation

The notion of the judgment of history rests on a progressive linear view about the necessary superiority, in every domain, of the future as compared to the past, but also—crucially—about the state as the political embodiment of that future. Massimiliano Tomba puts it nicely: "When Hegel made use of the concept of universal history, he placed the modern state at the tip of the historical-temporal arrow and worked backward, ordering every age in relation to the modern Western conception of freedom."[21] As articulated by Hegel, the "autonomy of the state" was "the ethical whole itself"—the modern state was at once the fulfillment and the embodiment of the telos of history. Tomba adds that the "state mechanism attempts to synchronize these temporalities," reducing multiple histories to a single, linear trajectory.[22] Koselleck connects the actions of the modern state to the eventual emergence of that new history. In its early formations, "the state enforced a monopoly on the control of the future by suppressing apocalyptic and astrological readings."[23] The political theorist Carl Schmitt, reflecting on politics and war, notes that for Hegel's epoch, "the state was the spatially concrete, historical organizational form, which, at least on European soil, had become the agency of progress."[24] He adds approvingly that "after the merciless bloodletting of religious civil wars, the European state and its bracketing of European land war into purely state war was a marvelous product of human reason."[25]

In Foucault's genealogy (a critique of Hegelian idealist representations), the modern state becomes a mode of being for itself and for its population; *raison d'état* constructs institutions of governmentality and subjects of the state: "To the great promise of the pastorate, which required every hardship, even the voluntary ones of asceticism, there now succeeds this theatrical and tragic harshness of the state that in the name of its always threatened and never certain salvation, requires us to accept acts of violence as the purest form of reason and of *raison d'Etat*."[26] With *raison d'état* comes a new temporality: "It is an indefinite temporality, the temporality of a government that is both never-ending and conservative. . . . The art of government and *raison d'Etat* no longer pose a problem of origin: we are always already in a world of government, *raison d'Etat*, and the state."[27] I would add that *raison d'état* is legitimated by its definition as (a humanly created) agency of progress, as the telos of history. And not just the telos (the internal directional drive of history), but its immutable instrument: "we are always already in a world of government, *raison d'Etat*, and the state."[28]

"'Statehood,'" Schmitt wrote, "is not a universal concept, valid for all times and all peoples. Both in time and space, the term described a concrete historical fact. The altogether incomparable, singular historical particularity of this phenomenon called 'state' lies in the fact that this political entity was the vehicle of secularization. The conceptual elaborations of international law in this epoch had only one axis: the sovereign territorial state."[29] The state, a "marvelous" accomplishment of human reason, is the instrument that subsumed religion to its secular will, thereby giving rise to order among the "civilized" states of Continental Europe. I have written elsewhere of the ways in which the subsumption of the religious to the political was conceived in terms of gender: women were to religion what men were to politics.[30] In this view, the state, progress, and the necessary direction of history are as one, with white European men in the lead.

The presumption that the state was the ultimate culmination of history's forward-moving path characterized postcolonial political organization as well. Gary Wilder describes the way in which alternative visions of political organization at the end of the French empire—federated entities of different but equal partners—were defeated by proponents of state sovereignty and, as a result, were lost to view in subsequent unilinear historical narratives.[31] The resulting story, say Nicola Perugini and Neve Gordon (writing of sovereign self-determination as the goal of emergent postcolonial nation-states), presumes that "only after the collective enters the framework of the state does it become an active agent of history."[32] The conflation of the state and history, Judith Butler notes, is "the temporal framework that uncritically supports state power, its legitimating effect, and its coercive instrumentalities."[33] The military and the police are examples of such instrumentalities, but so is the administration of law and justice as both domestic and international matters. From this perspective, it is the state that serves as the last resort for appeals to justice: law, courts, and judges adjudicate—that is, as they weigh matters of right and wrong, their rulings are equated with the delivery of justice itself. The judgment of history, then, becomes inseparable from the judgments of the designated juridical/legal institutions of the state. Historical agency is located in these institutions of state power; alternative sources of history—the actions of dissenting or rebellious groups and individuals, actions that often forced the hand of state power—are subsumed in the master narrative that privileges the state and attributes progress to its laws.

When European states became nations around the time of the French Revolution, their history took on a new dimension. A nation was defined as a people, united by some essential commonality (language, history, skin color, culture). This new definition, Hannah Arendt argues, was a way to overcome internal divisions—of class or social status, especially. Arendt points out that the designation of France as a nation in 1789 made apparent a fundamental contradiction between the declaration of *universal* human rights and their restriction to a specific *peuple*, located within the boundaries of a sovereign nation-state. Non-members of the state, whether deemed enemies or merely non-nationals, did not have recourse to the protection of law; in effect, they had no rights, they were stateless and, as a result, maintains Samera Esmeir, effectively nonhuman.[34] People without a nation were people without history. Writes Arendt:

> While consciousness of nationality is a comparatively recent development, the structure of the state was derived from centuries of monarchy and enlightened despotism. Whether in the form of a new republic or of a reformed constitutional monarchy, the state inherited as its supreme function the protection of all inhabitants in its territory no matter what their nationality, and was supposed to act as a supreme legal institution. The tragedy of the nation-state was that the people's rising national consciousness interfered with these functions. In the name of the will of the people, the state was forced to recognize only "nationals" as citizens, to grant full civil and political rights only to those who belonged to the national community by right of origin and fact of birth. This meant that the state was partly transformed from an instrument of the law into an instrument of the nation.[35]

The concept of the nation, premised as it was on the homogeneity of a people, was expressed as nationalism, characterized by what Arendt calls "race-thinking," distinctions that made some "essential" difference a ground for exclusion from the national body. The racist dimension of nationalism solidified and amplified, she argues, with capitalist expansion into imperialist outreach. Us/them distinctions took the form of a more explicit racism. "Imperialism would have necessitated the invention of racism as the only possible 'explanation' and excuse for its deeds, even if no race-thinking had ever existed in the civilized world."[36] It was indeed in the name of "civilization," deemed the highest achievement of human history (a moral as well as a political and economic concept), that imperial powers justified their conquests. ("The White Man's Burden" and "the civilizing mission" were among the many justifications offered.)

The concept of the nation introduces a conflict into the vision of the state as the telos of history because nations carry with them different temporalities, different reasons for being (*raisons d'être*). As Arendt notes, the universalist premise of law that claims to rest on principles of *human* rights was necessarily compromised by the need to respect law's now nationally based (racist) sovereign specificities. International law, respecting the principle of nation-state sovereignty (in Schmitt's words, the "marvelous product of human reason"), was the attempt to resolve the conflict. The task of international law was to mediate the relations of sovereign states, but also to distinguish good states from bad. The bad were defined as aberrations or anachronisms, the good exemplified the ongoing progress of civilization. In this way, the operations of international law at once presumed and confirmed the state as the universal agent of history.

Organization of the Book

In the chapters that follow, I take up three cases to explore the different ways in which the idea of the state as the embodiment and enactment of the judgment of history operated. Political actors have understood themselves to be implementing or demanding a judgment of history. The cases are the International Military Tribunal at Nuremberg, Germany, in 1946; the Truth and Reconciliation Commission (TRC) in South Africa in 1996; and the centuries-long, ongoing demand for reparations for slavery in the United States.

In each of these cases, the role of the state as the ultimate source of history's judgment is in play. There is a similar logic operating in two of the cases in which an evil power (the National Socialist regime in Germany, apartheid in South Africa) is called to the bar in the name of its victims by a benevolent power or set of powers. The action takes the form of a judicial (Nuremberg) or quasi-judicial (TRC) procedure; the victims' claims are adjudicated for them in the only place where justice can be dispensed. When the focus is on the retributive or redemptive power of state institutions, the agency of the "victims" is entirely erased. In contrast, the reparations movements refuse this logic, taking the nation-state to account for its repeated failures to bring justice to the enslaved and their descendants. They expose the nation-state as complicit in the perpetuation of injustice and call for a rewriting of its history to document that fact. In the case of reparations, the agents of the judgment of history are not states, but those who have endured enslavement and its legacies.

The three cases do have in common the question of race as it defines a nation: the Holocaust is the paradigmatic evil—the crime against humanity—that unites the three. US Associate Supreme Court Justice Robert Jackson, the chief prosecutor at Nuremberg, promised to document and punish the "sinister influence" of National Socialism in a way that would make it at once unforgettable and unrepeatable. Desmond Tutu, head of the TRC, denounced apartheid as "so utterly evil, immoral, unbiblical and unchristian that it can only be compared with that equally evil system—Nazism."[37] One of the advocates for reparations for slavery, Randall Robinson, called slavery "an American holocaust" worse in the extent of its carnage than what the Nazis had wrought.[38] If the Holocaust has been ruled an unspeakable evil, these instances ought to be as well. They all belonged in the proverbial dustbin of history. In the progressive narrative presumed by these actors, the past marks the morally unacceptable and, in evolutionary terms, the errors or failures of "immature" or "uncivilized" human rationality are on display there as lessons for the present about what must be avoided in the future. Although the evil took different forms historically, it had in common race as the marker of national identity. Indeed, it is racism and its relation to the nation-state that are at the heart of all three cases.

Could the nation exist without racism at its core? At Nuremberg the issue was avoided by depicting the Nazis as anachronistic or extreme, a state like no other. In this way, the ethnonationalism that characterized those other nations lived on unchallenged in the wake of the Tribunal. Even as its members looked to a nonracial future in a new South Africa, the TRC was unable to address the structural issues—economic especially—upon which state-sponsored racial oppression had rested, thereby permitting inequality (a racialized capitalism) to persist despite the political enfranchisement of the majority black population. The reparations movements offer a counterpoint to these two cases. In contrast, they take racial inequality as foundational to American national identity, and call for a rewriting of US history attentive not to singular linearity or homogeneity, but to the plural operations of power and difference.

My aim is not to rehearse the entire contexts in which these cases are situated, but to explore the ways in which the appeal—at once moral and political—to the judgment of history was associated with the nation-state. If justice were to be realized, it was by means of juridical action; some notion of a state-sanctioned rule of law was tied up with the realization of the judgment of history. Nuremberg was a formal international tribunal whose role was literally defined by the chief prosecutor as enacting the final judgment of history. Victory in war had established the rightness of the cause; the tribunal's role was to document the evil that must now be forever consigned to the past. The TRC was a quasi-judicial body whose role was to bring to light the suppressed history of apartheid and thereby to create the shared memory upon which a new, nonracial nation would be based. In both cases, the juridical mode was employed to achieve justice. The movement for reparations for slavery in the United States refuses the juridical mode, calling instead for a different kind of accounting. Demands for reparations date to well before the Civil War and have endured (with more and less visibility) to the present. Indeed in just the past few years they have acquired new attention and influence. Their existence exposes not only the repeated failures of demands for justice from the nation-state, but also the association of law and violence at its core. This exposure insists not on an alternative to the institution of the nation-state, but on a revision of what has been taken to be the progressive story of American history.

Reparations movements (in the United States, as elsewhere) provide a radical challenge to progressive views of history and of the nation-state as history's highest achievement; instead, they demand a history that attends to regress, inequities of power, disappointment and loss, and the fractured experience—the plural temporalities of that experience—of a nation's diverse peoples. They suggest as well the need to rethink what it is we mean when we look to the redemptive power of history as consolation or motive for action. I will take up that challenge for my own thinking about history in the epilogue.

ON THE JUDGMENT OF HISTORY

1

The Nation-State as the Telos of History

Nuremberg, 1946

> Yes, it would be worthwhile to study clinically, in detail, the steps
> taken by Hitler and Hitlerism and to reveal to the very distin-
> guished, very humanistic, very Christian bourgeois of the twenti-
> eth century that without his being aware of it, he has a Hitler
> inside him, that Hitler inhabits him, that Hitler is his demon, that
> if he rails against him, he is being inconsistent and that, at bottom,
> what he cannot forgive Hitler for is not crime in itself, the crime
> against man, it is not the humiliation of man as such, it is the
> crime against the white man, the humiliation of the white man,
> and the fact that he applied to Europe colonialist procedures
> which until then had been reserved exclusively for the Arabs of
> Algeria, the coolies of India, and the niggers of Africa.
> —Aimé Césaire, *Discourse on Colonialism*

The International Military Tribunal at Nuremberg was the
formal judicial inquiry that began in 1946 into the actions
of former Nazi officials and some National Socialist organizations. The trial (one of several conducted at the time) was a literal enactment of a judgment of history that had come with victory in war; the war had delivered the verdict, the role of the
Tribunal was to put it into effect. In the words of the chief
prosecutor, US Associate Supreme Court Justice Robert Jackson, "This trial will commend itself to posterity as fulfilling
humanity's aspirations to do justice."[1] It not only meted out retribution to the evildoers, but also, by establishing a record of

their crimes, aimed to render Nazi "sinister influences" politically and morally unacceptable forever. But there was something of a contradiction between the injunction to remember and the need to forget, between securing the memory of Nazi crimes in order to prevent their recurrence and the work of closure sought by the Tribunal's proceedings. If the dustbin of history was a closed book, how might certain forms of memory nonetheless keep the book open—and with what effects? Was it only Nazi crimes and their victims that constituted that memory? Where and how did the actions of those who resisted figure in the repository of memory assembled by the Tribunal? The deliberations of the Nuremberg Tribunal featured benevolent nations delivering a judgment against an evil regime in the name of its victims. The advance of history is secured by those benevolent nation-states.

The Nuremberg trials "for the first time called history itself into a court of justice." So argues Shoshana Felman in an essay on Walter Benjamin. "The function of the trials was to repair judicially not only private but also collective historical injustices."[2] Their judgment would bring the revelation of the "meaning of history," forcing it to "take stock of its own flagrant injustices."[3] History, in this view, was both subject and object of judgment at Nuremberg. The death sentences handed down were meant symbolically to confirm that justice had been delivered by the victorious nations, even if no ultimate compensation were possible for the crimes that had been committed or any guarantee established that their underlying causes had been eradicated.

The Tribunal was the joint effort of the triumphant powers (Britain, France, USSR, United States), conceived as a demonstration of the effectiveness of international law to provide the basis for cooperative relations among sovereign nation-states. Every step in the process was meant to illustrate what "civilized" legal proceedings looked like. "We must never forget that the record on which we judge these defendants today is the record on which history will judge us tomorrow," Jackson said in his opening statement.[4] By adhering to the technical requirements of the rule of law, the Tribunal would establish its moral credentials. Jackson was adamant about holding a proper trial, despite objections from other world leaders, some of whom would have preferred summary executions. Citing Woodrow Wilson, he stated that the trial aspired to "give international law the kind of vitality which it can only have if it is a real expression of our moral judgment."[5] International law was the collective demonstration of the reason of state, universalist in its claim to prosecute crimes against humanity. Law was the expression of morality, the means by which justice was to be realized. The word *justice* carries connotations of both the juridical *and* the moral; here the two were conflated.

The court was tireless in establishing an "objective" historical record in order to deliver the "ultimate verdict of history." "We must summon . . . detachment and intellectual integrity to our task," Jackson exhorted his colleagues, pointing to reams of documents as well as live testimony detailing Nazi crimes. The aim was to disclose the evil in a way "so painstakingly and with such clarity that the world could never forget."[6] The documents established the indisputable record of individual guilt, the legal basis upon which punishment would be administered, even as Nazi organizations were also on trial and even as state institutions were deemed responsible for criminal policies. "The idea that a state, any more than a corporation, commits crimes is a fiction. Crimes always are committed only by persons."[7] The distinction between states and individuals may well have looked ahead to a rehabilitated Germany in the postwar era, a potential ally in the coming Cold War. It was not the German people,

Jackson said, but their leaders who were on trial. Yet despite the careful distinction between states and individuals, the court could not escape a certain ambiguity; it could not refrain from attributing the evils it was adjudicating to the German nation-state, even as those punished were its individual representatives. It was Germany, after all, that had violated the covenants of international law, Germany whose deeds needed to be exposed and condemned to prevent their return, Germany that had lost its place in the family of "civilized" nations.

The contrast between evil and civilized recurred in the course of the trial, reflecting the presumption that the forward march of history resulted in a civilization somehow free of all evil. "Germany" was the antithesis of the victorious nation-states; a collective guilt was attributed to its people. Ironically, this image of Germany—as a homogeneous totality—echoed the National Socialist representation of the state and its *volk*. Here the Tribunal's view of history as ultimately embodied in nation-states operated to occlude the fact that there were Germans who resisted or opposed Nazi oppression, who tried to stop the disaster that Hitler and his coconspirators were imposing.[8] If there were glimpses of such people and their actions in the documents assembled by the Tribunal, they were more often described as victims than as agents of history; they were victims on whose behalf the jurists had assembled to enact some form of retribution. This was a story of states as totalities, not as sites of perpetual political conflict.

Historians and political theorists have written a great deal about Nuremberg as it involved the technicalities of international law, the origin of theories of human rights, and the definition of crimes against humanity. They have parsed the language of "aggressive warfare," a term left deliberately vague in the London Charter (1945), which established the Nuremberg Tribunal.

Many have concluded, with the political theorist Judith Shklar, that the evidence of genocide (plans for the extermination of the Jews, films of concentration camps, horrific descriptions of medical experiments) became "the moral center of the case."[9] The court was acting in the name of these victims of Nazi evil. "The logic of law will never make sense of the illogic of genocide," concluded the historian Lawrence Langer.[10]

All of that may be true in retrospect, though it was precisely the logic of law that the Tribunal sought to follow. Indeed, one of the fascinating things in the trial record is the anxiety expressed by Justice Jackson and his colleagues about the precedents being set for the legal issues of nation-state sovereignty and *raison d'état* (the prevailing meanings of the rule of law). His impressive opening speech made up in eloquence what it lacked in coherence. Was Nazi Germany a nation-state by conventional historical standards? Yes and no. Were Nazi crimes against the Jews unique (a new category of "crimes against humanity"), or were they extreme variations of ordinary nationalism and militarism? What made them different? How is the line drawn between acceptable and unacceptable nation-state behavior in order to justify punishment? The various answers Jackson offered show that the line was anything but clear and that moral considerations took second place to the need to protect the sovereign rights of (European and American) nation-states, to insist on their standing as the source of justice for those deemed victims and as the sole instrument of the direction of history. In the end, the only certainty that could be offered was that a victory in war had established the right of the victors to impose history's judgment.

Jackson's preoccupation with national sovereignty rested on a long-standing belief that the state was the culmination—the end in the sense both of aim and of final destiny—of history.

This view took for granted that the (now) democratic nation-state was the apex of historical evolution and the instrument of justice. We might call it the unconscious underpinning of the way in which judgment was articulated at Nuremberg. How to reconcile the evils of the National Socialist state with this view of history?

Was the Nazi Regime a Nation-State?

Jackson had different answers to that question. Sometimes, he treated the Nazi state as a sovereign German nation. It was only because it transgressed the international order of nations (violating their sovereignty) that its actions became unacceptable. The international order was, historically, meant to regulate relations among "civilized" nations; at the end of World War I, the Kellogg-Briand pact attempted to establish norms for their interactions and for the disciplining of "savage" political entities. At other times, Jackson described the Nazis as one of those savage entities that had been transformed by outlaws into a criminal enterprise. Yet again, he described the Nazis as representing an anachronism that didn't warrant the same treatment as "civilized" (by which he meant European and American) nation-states. It was as if the Nazis had fallen into a state of nature, outside the boundaries of law. In all of this, his overriding concern was with the rights and rules of existing nation-states in the international order—it was the protection of *their* integrity and *their* future that was finally at stake in this trial. To the extent that the Tribunal itself was delivering the judgment of history, it served not only to indict the Nazi state, but also to represent the victorious nations as the incarnation of justice and morality (even when a realistic assessment of their limits was occasionally conceded).

WAS THE NAZI REGIME A NATION-STATE?
YES (AN EXTREME EXAMPLE)

If the Nazis were a national state, Jackson wanted it clear that the Tribunal's intervention did not violate respect for national sovereignty in general and did not involve moral judgments of their internal affairs. The principle of sovereignty outweighed concerns for human rights. (Here is an example of the contradiction Arendt noted, which I cited in the preface, between declarations of universal human rights and the need to respect the sovereign particularities of nations.) Early in his speech, he referred to the National Socialist party program, which, in the name of the German people, "made a strong appeal to that sort of nationalism which in ourselves we call patriotism, and in our rivals, chauvinism."[11] This was especially true in relation to minorities. "How a government treats its own inhabitants generally is thought to be no concern to other governments or of international society. Certainly, few oppressions or cruelties would warrant the intervention of foreign powers."[12] Jackson even acknowledged "some regrettable circumstances in our country in which minorities are unfairly treated."[13] Indeed, he went on, there would have been no interfering with the Nazi's treatment of the Jews had it not been for their external aggressions. "Let there be no misunderstanding about the charge of persecuting Jews. What we charge against these defendants is not those arrogances and pretensions which frequently accompany the intermingling of different peoples and which are likely, despite the efforts of government, to produce regrettable crimes and convulsions."[14] Indeed, Jackson ruled out consideration of Nazi prewar atrocities on these grounds. As Elizabeth Borgwardt comments, "There was no principle available that could capture the crimes of Kristallnacht in Germany and yet spare from scrutiny the lynching of thousands of African-Americans in the American south."[15] In fact, the man who coined the term *genocide* at the time of the Tribunal refused its application to the US treatment of African Americans. When a group presented a petition to the United Nations in 1951 titled "We Charge Genocide: The Crime of the Government Against the Negro People," Raphael Lemkin insisted that "racist legislation and the social practice of lynching had nothing to do with his concept of 'genocide'" and he dismissed the authors of the petition as "un-American" and probably communist.[16]

In this connection—and in contradistinction to it—a book by the law professor James Q. Whitman documents in stunning detail the importance for Nazi jurists and policy makers of American race law. America served as a model for addressing immigration, miscegenation, second-class citizenship, and segregation. Its "distinctive legal techniques" were carefully studied and, in some cases, implemented—although the Germans considered the one-drop rule for determining racial identity too harsh.[17] The treatment of Native Americans during the American conquest of the West was, however, a model for the German pursuit of *lebensraum* in the territories of Eastern Europe.[18] Whitman concludes that "American white supremacy, and to some extent Anglophone white supremacy more broadly, provided. . . . some of the working materials for the Nazism of the 1930's. . . . But in Nazi Germany supremacist traditions and practices acquired the backing of a state apparatus far more powerful than anything to be found in the world of the daughters of British Imperialism and far more ruthless than any that had ever existed in Europe west of the Elbe."[19] There was surely a difference between racial discrimination per se and "racial persecution carried to the point of extermination,"[20] but did that make the Nazi state an extreme example, or an exception to the policies and practices of other nation-states? Was Nazism a "historical parenthesis" (as Benedetto Croce had deemed Italian fascism), an unfortunate "accident" (as Friedrich Meinecke described it), or was it something else?

The opening speech of François de Menthon argued that racism was a peculiar characteristic of National Socialism. He condemned the "diabolical barbarism" of the Nazis: "This monstrous doctrine is that of racialism:. . . Race is the matrix of the German people. . . . The individual has no value in himself and is important only as an element of the race."[21] Racialism was "the gulf that separates members of the German community from other men. The diversity of the races becomes irreducible, and irreducible, too, the hierarchy which sets apart the superior and the inferior races. The Hitler regime has created a veritable chasm between the German nation, the sole keeper of the racial treasure, and other nations."[22] Race or "racialism," in other words, characterized only Nazi Germany; the hierarchy of difference that underwrote French colonialism (to take only the example of Menthon's nation) had nothing to do with race! What Menthon referred to as "the common heritage of western humanism" was defined as civilized and free of racism in contrast to the "barbarity" of the National Socialist regime.

Jackson made the case for National Socialism as both extreme example and exception in his opening remarks to the Tribunal. The treatment of the Jews was criminal, he said: "History does not record a crime ever perpetrated against so many victims or one ever carried out with such calculated cruelty."[23] But although "the avowed purpose [of Nazi action] was the destruction of the Jewish people as a whole, as an end in itself," it was also "a preparation for war, as a discipline of conquered peoples."[24] The destruction of the Jews "enabled the Nazis to bring a practiced hand to similar measures against Poles, Serbs, and Greeks" and so prepared the way for "the precipitation of aggressive war."[25] "The reason that this program of extermination of Jews and destruction of the rights of minorities became an international concern is this: it was a part of a plan for making illegal war."[26]

The violation of other nations' sovereignty was a central issue. In this thinking, crimes against humanity and aggressive warfare become synonymous—the nation-state was the unit under attack. German designs on European countries—the conquest of *lebensraum*—were taken to be the goal of Nazi plans to exterminate the Jews. Léon Poliakov, an assistant to the French diplomat Edgar Faure at Nuremberg, wrote (in 1951), "As soon as one surveys the whole ensemble of Nazi racial policy and practice, one perceives the true significance of the extermination of the Jews: as a warning sign of greater and more general holocausts to come."[27] These holocausts, in Eastern Europe, the Tribunal concluded, "were part of a plan to get rid of whole native populations by expulsion and annihilation, in order that their territory could be used for colonization by Germans."[28] Poliakov was appalled at the German designation of "conquered peoples" as "so-called 'inferior races,'" and the Russian representatives at Nuremberg denounced German "imperialism," but (as Aimé Césaire reminds us in the epigraph to this chapter) no connection was made, indeed none was perceived, to European conquests of "inferior races" in other parts of the world.

Jackson tacked back and forth between justifying and denouncing the monumental "savagery" of the Germans. There was a moral dimension that compelled other nations to act, lest by their "silence [they] would take a consenting part in such crimes."[29] But he quickly returned to the argument that it was preparation for aggressive warfare that constituted the crime, not the domestic treatment of minorities. Here we see him grappling with the fact—at once acknowledging and denying it—that, as Robert Meister puts it, state sovereignty "assumes the continuing existence of territorial rule by national states. . . .

[It] rests on the simultaneous existence and repression of the genocidal thoughts, both active and passive, that founded the nation."[30] Meister cites Michael Mann's thesis that "genocide is the dark side of the notion that legitimate rule by *the people* over territory presupposed the absence (physically or culturally) of *other peoples* occupying that territory."[31]

By associating genocide (crimes against humanity) with aggressive warfare, Jackson attributed the dark side of nationalism exclusively to Nazi evil. Repeatedly invoked during the trials, aggressive warfare was never clearly defined (the Kellogg-Briand pact of 1928 wasn't considered a binding-enough legal document), although it was a necessary concept for distinguishing German incursions across national borders from the legitimate violence of *raison d'état*. Jackson acknowledged that "it is perhaps a weakness of this Charter that it fails to define a war of aggression."[32] He offered "civilized warfare" as its acceptable counterpart; indeed, it was the contrast between criminal and civilized warfare that established the definition. If the Nazi nation-state was a nation-state, it had lost its claim to sovereignty by violating international conventions; planning and waging "aggressive" warfare were criminal. The implied antithesis of aggressive was defensive. Said Jackson, "honestly defensive war is not a crime."[33] But he also sanctioned something beyond defensive war when he wrote: "War necessarily is a calculated series of killings, of destructions of property, of oppressions. Such acts unquestionably would be criminal except that International Law throws a mantle of protection around acts which otherwise would be crimes, when committed in pursuit of legitimate warfare."[34] By definition, legitimate warfare was "civilized," "aggressive warfare" was not. Or, to put it another way, the warfare of "civilized" states was legitimate, that of "barbarians" was not. This is the rationalization of warfare that Carl Schmitt attributed to the emergence of European states.

"Such wars," he wrote approvingly of these state wars regulated by international law, "represent the highest form of order within the scope of human power."[35]

The London Charter listed aggressive warfare as one of the counts against the Nazis. It was signed by the Allies on August 8, 1945, the day the United States bombed Nagasaki, two days after the bombing of Hiroshima; in February, the British and Americans had firebombed the city of Dresden— many thousands of civilians were killed in those raids. As for intervention in another sovereign nation, the Soviets had invaded Finland, Poland, Romania, and the Baltic states; Britain had invaded Norway. (Nothing was said about the long history of unprovoked imperialist incursions into Africa, Asia, Latin America, and the former Ottoman territories. Imperialism was assumed to be a right of these nations, the forward motion of the civilizing process.) Were these defensive operations or instances of aggressive warfare? And was it possible to insist that all war was a crime? The French prosecutor, François de Menthon, didn't think so; perhaps recalling Clausewitz ("politics is war by other means") he pointed out that "war was what states do."[36] The historian A. J. P. Taylor, referring to the documents assembled by the prosecution, noted that they "were chosen not only to demonstrate the war-guilt of the men on trial, but to conceal that of the prosecuting Powers."[37] It is in that light that we might read Jackson's distinction between civilized and criminal warfare, the one attributed to the victors, the other to the losers; the one the prerogative of legitimate states, the other outside the boundaries established by custom and covenant. It is in that light, too, that we might read the omissions necessary to constitute the moral certitude and the inherently progressive nature of the judgment of history being rendered by the nations staffing the International Tribunal.

WAS THE NAZI REGIME A NATION-STATE?
NO: IT WAS AN ANACHRONISM

Even as he insisted that no precedent was being set for the treatment of other nations, Jackson also denied that Germany under Nazi rule was a nation-state at all; it was not an extreme example, but an exception—for a number of reasons. First, the authentic German nation had been captured by a band of criminals—among them the individuals whose cases were before the Tribunal.[38] The National Socialist party was not in any sense a political party, even if its leader had been elected to office: "In discipline, structure, and method . . . [it] was not adapted to the democratic process of persuasion. It was an instrument of conspiracy and of coercion"—in short a criminal organization comprising "overlords" and their followers.[39]

The question of individual responsibility for state crimes became a precedent of the Nuremberg trials, although it raised difficult challenges to ideas about the limits of obedience to national rule—When did that rule become criminal and who was to judge? When did the sovereign autonomy of the nation-state demand respect? When did it exceed its boundaries? For the purposes of Nuremberg, the planning and implementing of aggressive warfare—violations of the sovereignty of other nation-states, allied with crimes against humanity—became the test; the scale was international, not domestic. But what counted as acceptable applied only to other established "civilized" nation-state entities; the colonial appropriation of nonstate territories didn't count as unacceptable "aggressive warfare"—even though the violent appropriation of land and people was certainly aggressive, as is evident in Schmitt's description: "The power of indigenous chieftains over completely uncivilized peoples was not considered to be in the public sphere; native use of the soil was not considered private property. . . . The land appropriating state did not need to respect any rights to the soil existing within the appropriated land unless these rights somehow were connected with the private property of a member of a civilized state belonging to the order of interstate, international law."[40] Imperialism was a matter of civilizing the natives, bringing them into the forward march of history.[41]

When the state-ness of Nazi Germany was denied, brigandage was a frequent description, evoking gangsters operating outside the law. Brigandage suggested that it was not states but only individuals (or gangs of them) who committed crimes. "The principle of individual responsibility for piracy and brigandage, which have long been recognized as crimes punishable under International Law, is old and well established. That is what illegal warfare is."[42] Here, by definition, legitimate nation-states cannot commit criminal warfare; the violence associated with *raison d'état* and the rule of law remains intact.

Individual responsibility was a major theme of the trial: statesmen who had "used their powers of state to attack the foundations of world peace" had to be brought before the law and made to "pay for it personally."[43] The theme was taken up dramatically in the film *Judgment at Nuremberg* (1961), released to coincide with the Eichmann trial in Jerusalem. With a star-studded cast (Spencer Tracy, Burt Lancaster, Richard Widmark, Marlene Dietrich, Judy Garland, Maximilian Schell, William Shatner, Werner Klemperer, Montgomery Clift), the question of individual responsibility is at the heart of the drama that focused on the Nazi lawyers who wrote and enforced the Nuremberg Laws of 1935. After all the complexities of cause and culpability are explored, clips of concentration camp victims shown, and the argument aired many times by the defense that patriotism required obedience to the laws of the nation, one German jurist acknowledges his guilt, but insists he never knew it would "come to this" (the Holocaust). The chief prosecutor's reply sums up the film's message: "Herr Janning, it came to that the first time you sentenced a man to death you knew to be innocent." In the end, individual men are responsible for their acts; the rule of law can be applied only to individuals. Echoing Jackson's words at the first of these trials, the movie prosecutor (Spencer Tracy) says that "civilization is the real complaining party." If individuals were responsible, nation-states were not; the rule of law thus stood inviolate. Putting the onus for violence on individual criminals, whose moral compass should have made them act otherwise, allowed the question of *raison d'état* to be put aside.

The failure to take responsibility was attributed to the abnormality of the Nazis: they were depicted as demented, deluded, psychotic. The pathology of individuals was at once cause and effect of a perverse regime. Lecturing to a popular audience, Hans Morgenthau noted that "Germany has been compared to a mental patient, a problem child, . . . a case of retarded development, or a young girl led astray."[44] Jackson referred to "diabolical barbarism," an evil that he said was fundamentally anti-Christian.[45] Christianity, in his view, was associated with a commitment to moral conduct and to peace; Christianity was taken to be the moral underpinning of modern secular European nation-states.

Yet another explanation offered for the rise of National Socialism was historic underdevelopment (as in Morgenthau's reference to "a case of retarded development"). It was the most frequent explanation given for the pathology of Nazi Germany; Germany could not be considered a modern state by the standards of the evolution of civilization. Some of the prosecutors pointed out that there were traces in Nazi character of the "youthful primitivism of the German spirit," and of "the primitive barbarity of ancient Germany."[46] In this they were an archaic remnant of another age, a relic of the state of nature for which the founding of states and nations had been a cure. Whitney Harris, who had served on the staff of the US prosecutor, noted in his history of the trial, published in 1954: "Despotism no longer has any place in civil society.... It is archaic, and of other times.... The age of empires has passed. And the time of emperors is gone"—thereby ruling out Western imperialism (by no means long passed) in the catalogue of despotisms.[47] Despotism belonged to the East: Jackson considered that Germany was "more Oriental than Western"; it had engaged in a "despotism equaled only by the dynasties of the ancient East."[48] Its alliance with Japan proved the Eastern connection: "they were brothers under the skin."[49] It was now time to relegate this remnant of past times to the dustbin of history; with the conviction of the Nazi defendants, evil would be permanently left in the past and the future progress of humanity (the defense of human rights as the expression of justice) would be assured by the laws of existing nation-states. There was no need to await a future judgment of history; the Tribunal was enacting it in the present.

Interestingly—and not surprisingly—the argument about German underdevelopment was echoed by some historians and commentators attempting to account for the Nazi state as an anomaly, a deviation from the normal process of state formation. This is not the place to go into the details of the *Sonderweg*—the argument that Germany had followed a special path, some maintained since the time of Luther, others only since the nineteenth century. Its deviation from the linear direction of history only served to confirm what was the true path. William Shirer, for example, wrote that Germans were predisposed to militarism and to the call of authoritarian leaders: "the course of German history ... made blind obedience to temporal rulers the highest virtue of Germanic man and put a premium on servility."[50] There were historians who diagnosed the Third Reich as a symptom of the rejection or failure of modernity, those who pointed to the persistence of preindustrial economic norms or to the discrepancy between industrial development and the emergence of a substantial middle class, those who cited the absence of a successful bourgeois revolution. Max Weber wrote of the "feudalization" of the upper bourgeoisie. Ralph Dahrendorf put it this way: German society "did not become bourgeois, but remained quasi-feudal. Industrialization in Germany failed to produce a self-confident bourgeoisie with its own political aspirations. . . . As a result, German society lacked the stratum that in England and America, and to a lesser extent even in France, had been the moving force of a development in the direction of greater modernity and liberalism."[51] This depiction of Germany's deviant development (as compared to the United States, France, and Britain) contributed to and followed the lines of distinction evident in the Nuremberg trial. There is one path that history takes: whether called civilization or modernity, its highest form is the (liberal democratic) nation-state. In this story, nation-states are treated as totalities rather than as products of political conflicts and contests. The results of these contests become reified as stages of historical development, rather than what they are—contingent instantiations of relationships of power. Moreover, these histories set aside what Jackson at least glancingly acknowledged: the role of nationalism in the process of state formation. The phenomenon of nationalism, the ways in which national identities are constituted as modes of inclusion and exclusion, did not figure prominently—if at all—in the analyses offered by these commentators.

Critiques of nationalism did figure, of course, in the writing of many others, Hannah Arendt a key theorist among them. She wrestled with distinctions between "mere nationalism and clear-cut racism." Genuine nationhood she deemed a belief in "the equality of all peoples" who shared some geographic frontier or history. The view of a history, she wrote, for which "every race is a separate, complete whole was invented by men who needed ideological definitions of national unity as a substitute for political nationhood."[52] In her account of it, what we now call ethnonationalism was a perversion of "genuine [political] nationhood," and the Germans were not the only source of the racial thinking it inspired.

The Survival of Ethnonationalism

I have been arguing that Nuremberg's treatment of Nazism—as a remnant of an earlier barbaric age—sought to protect a moral vision of the nation-state as the realization and agent of the judgment of history that nonetheless carried with it the possibilities for its recurrence. In the wake of the trials, important commentators had suggested as much. For example, Adorno pointed out in 1959 that "national socialism lives on, and even today we still do not know whether it is merely the ghost of what was so monstrous . . . or whether it has not yet died at all, whether the willingness to commit the unspeakable survives in people as well as the conditions that enclose them."[53]

Among those "conditions that enclose them," I would argue, is the form legitimated by the trial itself: the nation-state as the highest achievement of human political organization; *raison d'état* as the expression of sovereignty; "civilized" violence as the expression of sovereign state reason; and, especially, ethnonationalism as an exclusionary principle of membership in the nation-state. It may be that there are different types of nationalisms—benign as well as malignant—but a pernicious ethnonationalism seems to be increasingly the dominant one that accounts for the uncanny return of a banished "evil" in Charlottesville and elsewhere (including Germany).

Arendt was prescient about the dangers of "race-thinking" for "political nationhood" when she wrote critically of the founding of the state of Israel:

> After the war it turned out that the Jewish question, which was considered the only insoluble one, was indeed solved— namely by means of a colonized and then conquered territory—but this solved neither the problems of the minorities nor the stateless. On the contrary, like virtually all other events of our century, the solution of the Jewish question merely produced a new category of refugees, the Arabs, thereby increasing the number of stateless and rightless by another 700,000 to 800,000 people. And what happened in Palestine within the smallest territory and in terms of hundreds of thousands was then repeated in India on a large scale involving millions of people.[54]

Writing about the postwar regime of human rights (one of the direct results of the Nuremberg trials), Nicola Perugini and Neve Gordon endorse Arendt's view: "The same form of political organization that was historically responsible for the most egregious human rights violation was, in turn, elevated to the protector of human rights."[55]

Even with the caveat that the rules of international law are meant to restrain the worst impulses of nations, that nation continues as an autonomous entity enforcing its domestic (private) rules. The particular concern of Perugini and Gordon (like Arendt) is Israel, where they demonstrate that the protection of Jewish human rights has come at the expense of Arab human rights. During the Eichmann trial—which asserted the sovereignty of the new nation of Israel, acting in the name of the long history of the victimized Jewish people—"the Holocaust's threat was projected into Israel's current present and into a new territorial setting different from the one in which it had originated."[56] With the subsequent "nazification" of Arabs, Israel's "conquest and colonialization were normalized and legitimized as a sort of preemptive measure against the rematerialization of Auschwitz."[57] Even as "never again" justified these measures, Jews were defined as potential victims in need of the protection of the Israeli security state. And, in an ironic twist, the achievement of their place in history came, for the Jewish victims of the Nazi genocide, in the form of an ethnically defined nation-state, which (as the quotation from Michael Mann I cited earlier maintains) rests on "the notion that legitimate rule by *the people* over territory presupposed the absence (physically or culturally) of *other peoples* occupying that territory."[58]

This insistence on ethnic homogeneity as the fulfillment of a people's history is not peculiar to Israel but is, as Wendy Brown has shown, increasingly the way in which national identity is being defined in the face of globalization. She explains the frenzied building of walls by states across the world as a response to declining political sovereignty in the new global capitalist economic order, and she notes that this decline has unleashed the powers of "capital and religiously legitimated violence."[59] I would add ethnic and nationalist legitimated violence to that list: the desire to secure sovereignty by protecting and delimiting the homogeneity that establishes who counts as a member of a nation seems to have returned with a vengeance in the face of the so-called crisis of immigration confronted by the nation-states of the West.

The legacy of Nuremberg, then, was not only the documentation and denunciation of the worst ways in which the nation-state form could be realized (and I want to be clear here that, unquestionably, genocide constitutes an extreme form of ethnonationalism), but also a refusal to question the ethnonationalism (the racism) at the heart of the form itself.

The difference established between past and present was formulated in terms of different state forms: the one morally unacceptable (and so consigned to the past); the other taken to be the fruit of a progressive history (and so the fulfillment and the agency of history's judgment). In the framework of Nuremberg, the enduring fact of the nation, of a world of nations, was indisputable; the belief that law was a reliable instrument of moral justice was confirmed; the representation almost exclusively as victims of those who experienced Nazi rule underscored the importance of "good" nation-states and their laws as the primary agencies of history and justice; and the ongoing practices of racism were occluded by ascribing them to Nazi extremism, which, with the execution of its enactors, would—it was expected—finally be laid to rest. At Nuremberg, the defense of human rights was established as the job of "progressive" nation-states. In the juridical logic that prevailed, benevolent nation-states rescued or protected victims from evil, thereby establishing themselves as the agents of the judgment of history.

2

The Limits of Forgiveness

South Africa's Truth and Reconciliation Commission, 1996

One could never, in the ordinary sense of the words, found a politics or law on forgiveness.

—Jacques Derrida, *Forgiveness*

When the Truth and Reconciliation Commission (TRC) was established in 1996, its mandate explicitly rejected the "Nuremberg model." Although any number of commentators likened apartheid's implementation of ideologies of racial supremacy to those of the Nazi regime, they all rejected the idea that criminal trials were an option. The end of apartheid did signal a clear judgment of history: an evil regime was to be replaced by a more progressive democratic government. But retributive justice was simply not conceivable when there were no winners and when key institutions of the state were still in the hands of the oppressors. In the difficult negotiations that followed, what I referred to in the last chapter as a juridical logic, in which the victims of evil states are redeemed by the institutions of a benevolent state (or states), characterized the TRC's attempt to enact the judgment of history. The terms of negotiation, however, limited the possibilities for what could be done.

Negotiated Settlement

The period between 1989–90—the unbanning of the African National Congress (ANC) and the release from prison of Nelson Mandela—and Mandela's election as president in 1994 was the most violent in the history of apartheid.[1] Agents of apartheid remained in place at all levels of government and they did not give up power easily. Even as they negotiated an interim constitution, the National Party (NP) leadership unleashed its forces in the townships and the cities and enlisted the Inkatha Freedom Party (IFP) to attack its ANC rivals, claiming that black-on-black violence was the real threat to the nation. Chris Hani, head of the armed struggle branch of the ANC (which had called off its warfare now that a new order was at hand), was assassinated in 1993 by two white activists, who hoped, they said, to foment race war and thus prevent what they believed would be a communist takeover of the country.[2] Still controlling the parliament, the NP legislators passed a series of indemnity acts; some of them covered all parties to the conflict, others, secretly decreed by the president, applied only to state agents who were granted impunity for actions that had exceeded the bounds of legality even under the old regime.[3] At the same time, there were revelations of the torture and killing of suspected spies at ANC camps in exile.

"While the Allies could pack up and go home after Nuremberg, we in South Africa had to live with one another," explained the Anglican bishop Desmond Tutu, the chair of the TRC. "Neither side could impose victor's justice because neither side won the decisive victory that would have enabled it to do so, since we had a military stalemate."[4] The state security forces, Tutu noted, "still had the guns . . . and never would have negotiated if they had to face trial."[5] A negotiated settlement between the enforcers of apartheid and the resistance movements thus required pragmatic measures that would enable the two warring sides to find some common ground.

Although the TRC report referred to its moment as the last chapter in the struggle for African decolonization, it faced a different scenario from the one encountered earlier by many other national liberation movements. In South Africa, the colonizer remained on the scene with no intention to leave, having relinquished political domination but neither military nor economic power. The state form was in place, an institutional given that had to be reformed, but not overthrown. Yet its organs of justice were so corrupted that they could not be used to render judgment. There was no possibility of bringing the apartheid leaders to trial, no possibility of punishment, even if, in the eyes of the world, their actions constituted crimes against humanity. The defeat of apartheid was clearly a progressive historic accomplishment, but how to enact a judgment of history in these circumstances? That was the challenge the Truth and Reconciliation Commission faced.

The name of the Commission offered something of an answer: it would summon witnesses—victims—to recount their experiences and in that way document the truth of the old regime: history's truth would ultimately provide a memory and a moral judgment meant to serve a political end. Part of that end was to present the successor state to apartheid as the benevolent advocate/protector of apartheid's victims. It was their suffering at the hands of an evil regime (and not their agency as resisters) that was emphasized. The exposure of truth would set the terms not for retribution (as at Nuremberg), but for reconciliation; forgiveness in the light of the truth revealed was seized upon as the alternative to punishment. It would redeem the nation and ensure that South Africa's future was in step with the progress of history. The TRC was established to ensure the memory of apartheid—the things that had happened must not be forgotten. Yet its call to victims to forgive what they had suffered implied the need to forget. If forgiveness did imply forgetting, some argued, they would be experiencing a double loss: first, the death in struggle of their family or comrades and, now, the loss of that death to history.

The Commission adhered scrupulously to the rule of law, demonstrating the contrast between its commitments and those of the oppressive apartheid regime. In this way it operated as a quasi-judicial body. On the one hand, the TRC functioned like a court when it deposed witnesses, and when it considered and granted requests for amnesty. On the other hand, since it lacked the ability to punish, its authority was limited to moral counsel: forgiveness was endorsed as an individual response to the crimes being exposed. Jacques Derrida described the TRC as exhibiting a "confusion between the order of forgiveness and the order of justice," the one an individual's unconditional offering, the other the prerogative of the state or its representatives.[6] For forgiveness to be meaningful, Derrida says, it must be unconditional, beyond any sovereign power and with no instrumental purpose; forgiveness can have nothing to do with judgment. It is not a matter for law or the state. "Forgiveness remains heterogeneous to the order of politics or of the juridical as they are ordinarily understood."[7] He cites Tutu's account of the testimony of a woman who refused the Commission's request to forgive the murderers of her husband. "A commission or a government cannot forgive. Only I, eventually, could do it. (And I am not ready to forgive.)"[8] Derrida goes on to point out that the woman may also be suggesting that it is not her place to forgive; only her dead husband has that right. If forgiveness means somehow forgetting the sin, her action amounts to his double death. As a survivor, she cannot substitute for him, even if she is a victim as well. "Pure and unconditional forgiveness," he writes, cannot be reduced "to amnesty or amnesia, to acquittal or pre-scription, to the work of mourning or some political therapy of reconciliation."[9]

The confusion Derrida diagnoses "between the order of forgiveness and the order of justice," I think, was symptomatic of the impossible task the TRC faced: to effect national reconciliation—a political imperative—by moral means alone. The proceedings of the TRC were meant to enact a judgment of history and, in one sense, it succeeded in definitively establishing the criminality of the apartheid regime. But, in another sense, its focus on the rule of law applied to individuals and on forgiveness to be granted by individual victims limited the analysis of the very operations of history, and so the solutions it could offer.

Gramscian Catharsis or Christian Forgiveness?

Among the TRC's proponents there were two different con-ceptions of how to shape the new South Africa, one Marxist, the other Christian. Both rested on the idea that subjective transformation was a prerequisite to social, economic, and polit-ical change, but one sought to produce collective conscious-ness of oppressive structures, the other appealed to individual psychology.

The idea for the TRC came from Kader Asmal, a human rights scholar and political activist. Inspired by Latin American precedents from the 1980s and by Gramsci's notion of cathar-sis, Asmal saw the Commission as a means of effecting collec-tive subjective transformation.[10] For Gramsci, catharsis was "the starting point for all the philosophy of praxis." The politi-cal theorist Peter Thomas notes that according to Gramsci, "the philosophy of praxis was not concerned to exercise 'hegemony

over subaltern classes,' but, on the contrary, to encourage the
subaltern classes 'to educate themselves in the art of government,' thus making the 'ruled' intellectually independent from
the rulers."[11] Not the production of victims, but of agents—that
was the goal of catharsis. It was in this sense that Asmal wrote
that "the Truth and Reconciliation Commission should be a
final cathartic dam-burst, unleashing tides of reconstruction."[12]
The process worked by recounting the lived experiences of the
system's victims in order not to confirm their victimhood but
to expose in concrete detail the "truth" of a history, holding
accountable the white minority that either denied or did not
fully comprehend it. "The gist of genuine reconciliation is that
apartheid's beneficiaries must be persuaded to accept unwel-
come facts about their past."[13] "In the political context, reconciliation is a shared and painful ethical voyage from wrong to
right, and also a symbolic settling of moral and political indebtedness."[14] The testimony would come from "the previously
excluded [who] speak at last for themselves and . . . join the South
African family for the first time."[15] Their testimony would provide insight into the structural operations of power as they were
practiced under apartheid. "The South African Truth Commission is only one of the structures through which we should
hope to dismantle the old regime of truth in order to replace it
with new and multiple narratives."[16] The point was to create a
collective understanding of the structures that produced individual experience. "Reconciliation, accurately conceived, must
bring about a rupture with the skewed ethics of apartheid, and
so upset any possibility of smooth sailing on a previously
immoral course."[17] Asmal's goal was to expose the inequalities
of power that had led to the liberation struggles and that those
struggles had challenged. He expected that the TRC's revelations would enable the now enfranchised black majority to
"make history," finding its way to a new "reason articulating

system" that would redress the imbalance, enabling the creation of alternative forms of politics and law. For Asmal, this would be a "heterotopia" of "multiple idealisms forged from the diverse narratives that together produced a shared memory."[18] "The creation of shared memory . . . is not post-apartheid *volk* or a stifling homogeneous nationhood; nor a new Fatherland. . . . Shared memory, in the intended sense, is a process of historical accountability."[19] Historical accountability meant assigning responsibility for past injustice, recognizing the agency of opponents of the system, and changing the structures of power that enabled it in order to prevent its recurrence.

Asmal's vision was quickly eclipsed (and lost to many subsequent histories) by the teachings of the Anglican archbishop Desmond Tutu, who became the dominant voice of the TRC. Tutu's emphasis on individual responsibility contrasted sharply with Asmal's notion of collective consciousness. In his writings and in the Commission's Report, Tutu stressed individual experience; he talked (in the language of medicine and psychoanalysis) of the trauma victims had suffered, of the need to heal their psychic wounds. In the definitions established by the TRC under his leadership, victims were those with direct experience of harm in the time frame of the Commission's deliberations (1960–94), not the collective targets of apartheid's oppressive social and political rule.

For Tutu, the TRC was a "deeply theological and ethical initiative."[20] He defined the work of the Commission as promoting forgiveness—the forgiveness exemplified by Jesus, and also (to strike a culturally appropriate note) the forgiveness inherent in the African notion of *ubuntu*, an understanding of the self as inextricably bound up with others: forgiveness is offered by the victim to redeem the sinners of their sins. Although the crimes to be forgiven were unforgiveable—those murdered and tortured could never be restored or made whole—Tutu's forgiveness confused (in Derrida's words) "a judicial logic of amnesty" with a "therapy of reconciliation."[21] It was symptomatic of the dilemma the TRC faced.

Under Tutu's leadership, forgiveness was indeed therapeutic; it was promoted as a work of mourning that sought to establish normality in a country rent by civil war. As an instrument of politics, it was profoundly depoliticizing, turning attention away from Asmal's structures of power to the status of individual souls. Tutu maintained that "the act of telling one's story" had a "cathartic, healing effect."[22] But his notion of catharsis had less to do with establishing political agency than it did with purging individual passions of anger and sorrow—those passions that had, in fact, fueled the political agency of the liberation movement. When a judge granted amnesty (in effect forgiveness) to the murderers of the ANC activist Steven Biko, he defended the action by pointing to the need to construct a "historic bridge" to democracy: "If the Constitution kept alive the prospect of continuous retaliation and revenge, the agreement of those threatened by its implementation might never have been forthcoming and, if it had, the bridge itself would have remained wobbly and insecure, threated by fear from some and anger from others."[23]

The TRC publicized dramatic moments of forgiveness (e.g., the mothers of murdered boys forgiving their police assailants) as a way of stressing the imperative to staunch the desire for vengeance with the balm of forgiveness.[24] "We cannot go on nursing grudges even vicariously for those who cannot speak for themselves any longer," Tutu warned.[25] Here he implies the need not only to forgive, but to forget. "Forgiveness is letting go of your right to retaliation. It is like opening a window to let the fresh air rush into a dank closed room, it is drawing the curtains apart to let the light stream into a dark room."[26] (The idealization of Mandela exclusively as a man of peace and forgiveness—and not, at one time, the supporter of armed struggle—was an effect of this kind of thinking.) The pathologization of anger not only aims to calm agitated spirits, but implies as well the need to forget its object: the injustices and unpunished crimes of agents of apartheid. It also delegitimizes the anger that was one of the motives for the liberation struggle and its historic role in securing the end of the evil regime.

But justifiable anger was, after all, what had helped fuel the liberation movement; for some of its members the call to forgiveness seemed a call to forget. A woman named Kalu criticized the TRC this way:

> What really makes me angry about the TRC and Tutu is that they putting pressure on me to forgive. . . . I don't know if I will ever be able to forgive. I carry this ball of anger within me and I don't know where to begin dealing with it. The oppression was bad, but what is much worse, what makes me even angrier, is that they are trying to dictate my forgiveness.[27]

If forgiveness cancels anger, she suggests, it also denies its justification and so the memory of the history she has lived.

Despite objections of this kind, the TRC Report insisted on the importance of forgiveness. It concluded with these words: "It is only by recognizing the potential for evil in each one of us that we can take full responsibility for ensuring that such evil will never be repeated."[28] In this comment, the need to forgive the sinner refuses any structural account of how evil's potential is elicited, and it equates perpetrators and victims as equally vulnerable—differentials of actual power are beside the point. Asmal's notion of collective political consciousness becomes, in this representation, a series of horrific reminiscences that individual victims, and the nation as a whole, are asked to recall and to forgive (and then forget?), in order to move on. In the morality play staged by the TRC, the punishment dealt out to individuals at Nuremberg becomes the redemption (and so the reconciliation) of victimized and corrupted individual souls.

Historical Accountability

The reconciliation the TRC sought rested on the exposure of the truth of apartheid's brutal past. Truth emerged in the accounts of victims and the confessions of perpetrators. But would these constitute a consensus, a collective memory of a past (a history) that must be repudiated as a precondition for a more just future? Asmal thought so. Collective memory, he maintained, involved an analysis of apartheid as a system that produced its agents, its challengers, and its victims, an account of ideological and institutional struggles and structures of oppression. He cited the case of Bram Fischer to make his point. Born into an Afrikaaner family, Fischer eventually became one of the lawyers representing Mandela. His conversion from a "young apostle of segregation" to "a towering figure in the anti-apartheid movement" involved an analysis of the system of racial oppression, a recognition of the painful truth of apartheid. Asmal took Fischer to demonstrate the possibilities of a future nonracialist South Africa: here was a white man who "placed himself vigorously on the correct side of history at a time when that was a dangerous thing to do." That understanding of history would have to be imposed on those who had once supported the apartheid state: "In no sense can his [Fischer's] example be equated with the individual and collective responsibility that is borne by South Africa's passive beneficiaries and practitioners of apartheid. For them, coming to terms, after the fact, with their gainful complicity in the past will necessarily be a different process. But it remains an imperative."[29]

What would that process of "coming to terms" entail? Asmal wasn't clear about it and neither was the TRC. Was "historical accountability" the same as individual accountability? Yes and no. The TRC took as its mission the creation of the understanding that would encourage forgiveness (of the self and of others) and this revealed an often-contradictory notion of historical causality. Despite its evocations of the individual propensity to evil as the source of historical abuses, the Commission also repeatedly gestured to apartheid as a "system" of rule. "The apartheid system in South Africa was a crime against humanity, in spite of the fact that it was perfectly legal within that country, because it contravened international law."[30]

The Commission's Report began with an account of the history of apartheid, depicting it as colonialism's legacy and its excess. The testimonies it solicited added up to an indictment of the laws and customs of the white supremacist state. The TRC vision of the state of the future conceived it as the antithesis of the apartheid state, the fulfillment of justice as both a morally driven and an innovative legal/juridical project. Its recommendations, calling for the nurture and implementation of "a human rights culture," extended across the gamut of societal institutions both public and private.

Yet when it came to assigning responsibility for gross human rights violations, the "policies of apartheid" were gestured to only as "the broader context within which specifically defined gross human rights violations had taken place."[31] The emphasis instead was on the need for individual victims to forgive their oppressors and for individual perpetrators to avow their crimes. Few perpetrators came forward, certainly not the leadership of the apartheid state. This left it to the victims to forgive. The report put it this way: "A key pillar of the bridge between a deeply divided past of 'untold suffering and injustice' and a future 'founded upon the recognition of human rights, democracy, peaceful co-existence, and development opportunities for all' is a wide acceptance of direct and indirect, individual and shared responsibility for past human rights violations."[32] The structures within which "crimes against humanity" had been legitimated were not, as Greg Grandin (writing of earlier Latin American commissions) put it, "presented as a network of causal social and cultural relations but rather as a dark backdrop on which to contrast the light of tolerance and self-restraint."[33]

PERPETRATORS

In pursuit of historical accountability, the Commission sought to document the criminality, the lawlessness, and the vicious racism of the individuals who formulated and delivered the violent policies of the apartheid state. In the absence of official records (most either had never been kept or were destroyed as the end neared), the testimony of victims provided evidence, in horrific detail, of the human rights violations they had endured: their property stolen, their children slaughtered, their bodies defiled. The (very few) accounts by perpetrators (most of whom were minor figures in the state apparatus) were no less horrifying, even when (and often because) they were delivered with little or no affect, and even when they were justified as being in compliance with the orders of the apartheid state. All of this was televised to reach the widest possible audience—a guarantee, it was hoped, of the production of shared historical memory.

But the nature of that memory—as well as the notion of causality upon which it rested—was disputed by some of those designated as perpetrators. The chief enforcers of apartheid objected to the accusation that their past actions were crimes against humanity. The former president D. W. de Klerk insisted on this during the negotiations and again when he successfully petitioned a court to suppress parts of the Commission Report that documented his criminal actions.[34] He asserted that the future unity of the nation required "non-condemnation of past history" and "understanding" of the fact that diverse perspectives had informed the motives of the conflicting sides in the struggle.[35] De Klerk's moral relativism was echoed by the former NP member Wynand Malan, the one person on the TRC to dissent from its final report. He denounced the report for its "lack of empathy with certain groups living within traditional or nationalistic value systems who were party to the conflict."[36] They could not be blamed, he insisted, for adhering to the rules of another "value system." For de Klerk and Malan, there could be no judgment of (by? for?) history—that was an unacceptable moralizing. The only acceptable position was pragmatic adaptation to the present state of things. Adam Ashforth (writing about the political resonance of ideas of witchcraft) notes that for many South Africans watching this process, "the fact that the leadership of the NP failed to confess their full activities (including their secret activities) and their malicious motives is more than just a galling reminder of their stubborn shamelessness. The evil source of suffering remains alive and ready to strike again."[37] Put another way, history's judgment could not do the work of closure in these circumstances.

In the light of the resistance to historical accountability by some of the key players, the TRC turned ever more insistently to the importance of victims' forgiveness and to the need to stem the anger this resistance would inevitably produce in apartheid's victims. Even if they failed to acknowledge their crimes, a generous population, recognizing its own propensity to evil, might forgive them. History, after all, had already delivered its judgment of their crimes.

BENEFICIARIES

The TRC's attention to individual criminal responsibility drew a sharp distinction, as Robert Meister points out, between the passive beneficiaries of the system and its active enforcers. With it, the question of what counted as historical accountability came to the fore: Was it required only of those who actually killed and maimed, or also of those who assented to and benefited from the system of white minority rule? Did the prevalence of a different "value system" exempt individuals from culpability (as de Klerk and Malan insisted)? The TRC response (reflecting its refusal to directly take up the impact of structures on individuals) was exemplified by its explicit rejection of one woman's appeal for amnesty on the grounds of her acknowledged "apathy," that is, her "a lack of necessary action in time of crisis," her failure to actively oppose what she knew to be a criminal regime.[38] In the eyes of the Commission, there was no actual crime for which she could be forgiven.

In effect, the distinction between beneficiaries and perpetrators enacted the very general amnesty the ANC had opposed in negotiations with the NP, absolving of criminal responsibility those who had accepted pass laws and property confiscations as their legal entitlements, but who had committed no "gross violations," that is, no excessive or discernable harm to black bodies.[39] Since these people were said to have no victims, there could be no justified claims made against them. The criminality of the systemic violations against which the liberation movement had fought for decades and which were acknowledged (morally, abstractly) by the TRC was, in this way, in practice (legally, formally) denied since only individuals were held responsible for it.

And the motivation of the revolutionaries—to reverse their collective victimhood once and for all—was denied as well.

Writes Meister, "By accepting the distinction between individual perpetrators and collective beneficiaries of injustice as essential to the 'rule of law,' the formerly revolutionary victim becomes 'reconciled' to the continuing benefits of past injustice that fellow citizens still enjoy. He would thus appear 'undamaged' in the sense that he has now put his victimhood firmly in the past."[40] But it is not only his victimhood that is relegated to the past, but his heroic resistance as well. When resisters are defined primarily as victims, their agency (past and future) is compromised, if not lost. Meister argues that the repair of these damages meant relinquishing (or at the least infinitely deferring) some of the goals that revolutionary justice had sought to attain. "The rule of law in the aftermath of evil is expressly meant to decollectivize both injury and responsibility and to redescribe systemic violence as a series of individual crimes."[41] In this way some of the structures of inequality were left untouched, even as the wheels of a more equitable system of justice had begun to turn.

The Rule of Law

Adherence to the liberal ideal of the rule of law was a guiding principle for the TRC. The description of apartheid as a crime against humanity defined it as a violation of standards of international law. This had long been understood by observers and institutions such as the United Nations and the International Labor Organization; the liberation movements were not alone in their condemnation.[42] It thus was crucial that the juridical practices of the new South Africa restore the legitimacy of legal institutions, many of which had come to be associated with protecting the criminal violence of the apartheid state.

The rule of law, once openly violated by the white minority, was now invoked to acknowledge the humanity of the black majority by making them citizens of the new South Africa. Indeed, as Samera Esmeir argues (referring to postcolonial Egypt), in this way humanity and citizenship come to define each other; political rights are human rights. In South Africa, black citizens were now subjects of the law, effectively enfranchised by but also bound to the powers of the state. Esmeir points out that other ways of organizing justice disappear with the introduction of the modern rule of law: "The coloniality of the law is found in the forceful elimination of past legal traditions, in the conquest not only of a territory and it inhabitants but also of the past."[43] In the case of South Africa, many past practices of communal justice were put aside with the extension to black citizens of the rule of law. Although some alternative juridical forms in township communal deliberations have persisted to this day, the nation-state is the final arbiter of law and justice: in effect, the telos of history.

The TRC's mandate was addressed to "conflicts of the past," specifically to the years from 1960 to 1994, the period between the Sharpeville Massacre and the inauguration of Nelson Mandela as president. This was a long, thirty-year struggle pitting the liberation movements against an increasingly militarized and punitive regime; the narrow emphasis on these years of political conflict drew attention away from the longer history of apartheid (it dated at least to 1948) and the political, economic, and social structures it had put in place. Within the defined period of the TRC's mandate, there was also a narrow definition of what constituted political conflict. In the assessment of amnesty claims, for example, amnesty was offered only to those individuals said to have been acting on behalf of organizations explicitly advocating political conflict. The assassins of Chris Hani thus were refused amnesty on the grounds that the Conservative Party to which they had belonged and on whose behalf they had apparently acted did not have a policy advocating violence.

The liberal premises of the rule of law also required ignoring the power differentials (political and economic) established and enforced by state violence, that is, ignoring what Asmal had defined as the underlying "truth"—the structural truth—of apartheid. In the deliberations of the TRC, the infractions of ANC members were equated with those of the enforcers of apartheid. Tutu described this as the "even-handed" determination of victims, "because the political affiliation of the perpetrator was almost a total irrelevance in determining whether a certain offense or violation was a gross violation or not." It was the individual act that established the guilt. "Thus, there was legal equivalence between all, whether upholders of apartheid or those . . . who were seeking its overthrow."[44] Legal equivalence, he insisted, was, of course, not the same as moral equivalence; nevertheless, the condemnation of apartheid as a crime against humanity and the endorsement of the liberation struggle as a "just war in a just cause" did not obviate the need to enforce the rule of law as embodied in the Geneva Conventions. "A just cause must be fought by just means; otherwise it may be badly vitiated."[45]

But legal equivalence (between agents of the apartheid state and those who resisted it) effectively denied the history that the TRC was trying to document and the agency as resisters of the opponents of apartheid. Asmal, who had by now become a critic of the TRC, pointed out that the power imbalance in the apartheid state was the source of *all* the violence: "While decades of white supremacist violence assaulted the very ideas of the rule of law and constitutionalism, the anti-apartheid resistance was the dutiful safe-house of these ideals."[46] Moreover, he said, any violence committed by the ANC was a function of the apartheid

state and not of criminal individuals. "It needs to be empha-
sised again that the oppressed majority had no access to normal
democratic channels, no vote and no right to peaceful protest.
In these conditions, armed struggle was not a choice but a
necessity, a burden taken up with reluctance, but also with
integrity and dignity."[47] The occasional lapses that occurred, he
insisted, had to do with a few rogue members of the movement
and could not be compared with the systemic violence of the
apartheid state. Asmal was sharply critical of what he deemed "a
flexible book-keeper's version of history [that] would produce a
suspect balance sheet of alleged facts and opinions, a product of
free-form addition, subtraction or multiplication towards con-
venient conclusions, without deference to relevant realities." By
giving equal weight to "the Great Men who ran the system,
rather than to the perspectives of the victims and of those who
resisted the system on the ground," this approach "would sacrifice truth itself."[48]

Despite these objections, the Commission refused to locate
blame for all the violence in the state apparatus and its agents; it
held the liberation movements equally culpable, demanding
that they "issue a clear and unequivocal apology to each victim
of human rights abuses" and that they "seek to reconcile with
and reintegrate the victims of [their] abuses."[49] Richard Wilson
deemed this a "moral equalizing of suffering," and it followed
from strict application of the rule of law. "In the hearings, com-
missioners repeatedly asserted that all pain was equal, regard-
less of class or racial categorization or religious or political affiliation. Whites, blacks, ANC comrades, IFP members, and
others all felt (or caused) the same pain. No moral distinction
was drawn on the basis of what action a person was engaged in
at the time."[50]

In this way, reconciliation came to mean a minimizing, if not
a denial, of the unequal relations of power that characterized

the parties to the conflict. And it made all parties to the conflict responsible for their victims; the members of the liberation struggle and the agents of the apartheid state were deemed equally culpable. As history moved progressively from an evil past to a redeemed future, the focus was less on power dynamics and more on the shape and behavior of the state. The logic of evil state/victims/benevolent state prevailed. The conflict was decontextualized and depoliticized: the defenders and resisters were, in effect, denied their different histories. The imposition of the rule of law, taken to be objectively unconcerned with inequalities of power, was here at odds with the particular judgment of history that the repudiation of apartheid was meant to achieve. It also removed from the table scrutiny of the ongoing power imbalances and political differences within the new regime, especially in relation to the racialized capitalist organization of the economy.

LEGAL CONTINUITY I: INDEMNITY AND AMNESTY

In the transitional period during which the TRC operated, continuities of law seemed inevitable, as the ANC parliamentarian Johnny de Lange explained: "Since our transition entailed a gradual, though marked shift from one legal order to another, it necessitated the acceptance of legal continuity. In constitutional, legal and practical terms this meant that the apartheid legal order remain the law of the land, even if unconstitutional, until amended by the democratic parliament, or declared unconstitutional by the Constitutional Court."[51] In order to maintain the state form there could be no alternative to this kind of transition; the rules of governance might be rewritten, but— leaving aside the issue of the necessity of political compromise— the existence of the state as a sovereign entity had to be maintained.

Continuity, at least in the period of transition, required acknowledging past practices of indemnity, that is, accepting the way in which legality had been conferred on patently illegal acts. Adam Sitze describes it this way: "Indemnity acts did not so much legalize occasional illegalities as illegalize legality itself, allowing 'race war' to be prosecuted in the name of the 'rule of law.'"[52] This meant that many of those known to have committed "gross violations of human rights" could never be charged; they had already been legally excused. But there were others whose actions could be examined if they chose to recount them, and they might appeal for forgiveness to the Amnesty Committee of the TRC. In the negotiations, the ANC refused to grant blanket amnesty to apartheid's agents, insisting that individuals apply for it by confessing to their crimes—in this way the Truth would be established and, at the very least, the families of those killed, tortured, or disappeared might learn what had actually happened to them.

But there was an undeniable link between the apartheid state's indemnity and the TRC's amnesty, according to Sitze, and this had to do with "the jurisprudence of emergency" or necessity. Under apartheid, declarations of martial law in the name of national security were accompanied by acts of indemnity, exempting the illegal actions of "certain classes of persons . . . from criminal and civil liability." Amnesty was justified in the TRC by a similar necessity to keep the state intact ("but for an amnesty agreement, South Africa would have dissolved into civil war"). Writes Sitze, "Both genres of jurisprudence refer to situations in which the very existence of the state itself is in question and in which 'the necessity of saving the state from destruction' authorizes a swerve from or suspension of the normal procedures and practices of the rule of law."[53] Sitze suggests that the adoption of the necessity argument by the TRC was risky; in the name of healing the victims of apartheid, it imported into the new South Africa the very "discourse of martial law, which both authorized and incited many of the gross human rights abuses the TRC was mandated to investigate."[54] At the same time, what he terms the "genius" of the move might be realized if this was the last time such state powers were to be deployed. "It is whether or not the TRC's reiteration was sufficiently felicitous to institute a new mode of juridical reason— one capable of *completing* the crisis of colonial jurisprudence that occasioned the invention of the TRC to begin with."[55] Whether the new constitution's provisions, which explicitly ruled out indemnity for "the police or other security forces" "even under a state of emergency," would be enough to do this in the face of *raison d'état*—justifiable state violence in the name of stability, prosperity, and security—remained to be seen.[56]

LEGAL CONTINUITY 2: PROPERTY RIGHTS

A more discernable and lasting continuity had to do with property ownership. As part of the negotiated settlement, the bill of rights in the new constitution left in place established property rights. Their recognition was taken to be an instance of fealty to the rule of law, enshrined in the new constitution. But the assumed universal applicability of the rule of law clashed with the particular circumstances of its enforcement. Was property that had been acquired under apartheid laws which sanctioned theft, dispossession, and discrimination legitimately protected in the new regime? Asmal argued for an interpretation of the new constitution that would take this history into account. "We must keep in mind that property in the strict sense of a legitimate and settled entitlement, is very different from the pillaged belongings that many people took under apartheid. The right

to property now has a place in the final constitution. But prop-
erly understood the ideas of rectification and redress, not stasis,
are at the heart of the new, legitimate, concept of property."[57]

The TRC's final recommendations on this matter did not
follow Asmal's thinking. Instead, they defined the problem and
the solution in individual terms and they left the capitalist
organization of society in place. The TRC called upon the business community and local and regional governments working
with the Land Commission to "undertake an audit of all unused
and underutilised land, with a view to making this available to
landless people. Land appropriated or expropriated prior to
1994 should also be considered in the auditing process, with a
view to compensating those who lost their land."[58] But the Land
Commission (established in the 1990s) not only worked with
the idea of private property as a test of ownership (when communal property had often been the rule among local groups),
but was massively underfunded. The head of the commission
complained that "we are the Cinderella of the commissions. . . .
If the government will deny me the 20 million rand I need to do
my job . . . then they are not taking [land] restitution seriously."[59]
The result of this was, as Mahmood Mamdani puts it concisely:
"Where property rights clashed, as in the case of white settlers
and black natives, the former received constitutional protection, the latter no more than a formal acknowledgment in
law."[60] No amount of forgiveness could rectify this continuing
injustice.

The TRC did recognize an imperative of redistribution: "It
will be impossible to create a meaningful human rights culture
without high priority being given to economic justice by the
public and private sectors."[61] But redistribution could only come
from voluntary actions. The means of achieving "a meaningful
human rights culture" was ultimately a matter of individual
responsibility at the moral and material levels: "It is up to each

individual to respond by committing ourselves to concrete ways of easing the burden of the oppressed and empowering the poor to play their rightful part as citizens of South Africa."[62] Here the question is one not of securing economic equality, but of "easing the burden" and "empowering the poor" as citizens— that is, accepting the fact that the poor are "always with us" even when they have achieved formal political emancipation— the perfect neoliberal conceptualization. This state of things led one critic to comment that "Reconciliation was the Trojan horse used to smuggle unpleasant aspects of the past . . . into the present political order, to transform political compromise into transcendent moral principles."[63]

Here it might be useful to recall Karl Marx's critique of formal political equality based on abstract individualism, as at once the refusal and the reproduction of social inequality.

> The state abolishes, after its fashion, the distinctions established by birth, social rank, education, occupation, when it decrees that [these] are, non-political distinctions, that every member of society is an equal partner in popular sovereignty. . . . But the state, more or less, allows private property, education, occupation, to act after their own fashion, namely as private property, education, occupation, to manifest their particular nature. Far from abolishing these effective differences, it only exists so far as they are presupposed; it is conscious of being a political state and it manifests its universality only in opposition to these elements.[64]

In South Africa, we can see this concretely: the extension of political rights to the black majority left in place ("presupposed") long-standing social and economic inequalities. And race, as Wilson argues, was also taken to be not a structural problem, but a matter of individual attitude. Violence, he writes, was not defined as "the product of state structures and social inequality, but of 'political intolerance.' The *Report* also appealed to 'racism' as an explanatory category, but racism was not conceptualized in both institutional and experiential components, but instead as a set of values and sentiments held by individuals."[65]

Metaphors of the Bridge

Forgiveness was offered as the instrument of redemption, the way of equalizing the terrain upon which compromise and reconciliation would be achieved. It was often referred to as creating the conditions for a "bridge" to the future. "Forgiveness declares faith in the future of a relationship and in the capacity of the wrongdoer to make a new beginning on a course that will be different from the one that caused the wrong."[66] The bridge of forgiveness was the edifice in the present that would enable the coming into being of a new and better future. It was the state's instrument of reconciliation, the means of realizing and implementing the judgment of history.

The TRC's metaphor of the bridge described a one-way route, like a linear vision of history itself, from past (the apartheid state) to future (a new South African nation). Once it was crossed, those traversing it would arrive at the promised land. Asmal had spoken glowingly of a "heterotopia" of "multiple idealisms,"[67] forged from diverse narratives, that was not "a new Fatherland" of "stifling homogeneous nationhood."[68] Tutu cited Jesus: "'And when I am lifted up from the earth I shall draw everyone to myself.' . . . There is no longer Jew or Greek, male or female, slave or free—instead of separation and division, all distinctions make for a rich diversity to be celebrated for the sake of the unity that underlines them."[69] A nonracialist, rainbow nation awaited these tired time-travelers. But the bridge, the edifice of salvation, was not yet finished; it was under construction.

The TRC Report described its job as putting in place pillars that were part of a "process of bridge building."[70] Dullah Omar, the minister of justice in the interim government, described the legislation that created the TRC, the Promotion of National Unity and Reconciliation Act of 1995, as

> a pathway, a stepping stone, *towards the historic bridge* of which the Constitution speaks whereby our society can leave behind the past of a deeply divided society characterised by strife, conflict, untold suffering and injustice, and commence the journey towards a future founded on the recognition of human rights, democracy and peaceful co-existence, and development opportunities for all South Africans irrespective of colour, race, class, belief or sex.[71]

Amnesty—the forgiveness of individual criminal action in individual cases—was, in the words of the judge I cited earlier (who defended the procedure against claims by the family of the murdered ANC activist Steven Biko that it was unwarranted and unconstitutional), the mechanism by which the "historic bridge" to democracy would be constructed.

In effect, the bridge was the concrete embodiment of history, a history whose direction was necessarily emancipatory, though it required human action (the construction now taking place) for its realization. That idea of history had informed the liberation movements, not only in South Africa, but everywhere on the globe. It inspired leaders and their followers to dream of and act to achieve a better world. In South Africa, the bridge enabled the TRC to assume that the idealized nation it imagined would come about as a result of its efforts; but it also minimized the weakness of forgiveness as bridge-building material. In the metaphor of the unidirectional bridge, the future was in some sense assured by History; current difficulties would be resolved in the long run when the work of construction was complete. The full implementation of the judgment of history might be deferred for the moment in the light of the political realities of the negotiated settlement, but it would eventually prevail. After all, apartheid was over, a new political democracy was taking shape. This history was about the difference between past, present, and future.

But that notion of history assumes a starker separation between the time frames than is ever actually the case. And it underestimates not only the persistence of the past into the present and future, but also the enduring effects of political compromise and the structures that support it. The experience of the TRC and the impact of some of its actions seem to me to call for a different metaphor of the bridge as an operation of history. The one I want to offer comes from Michel de Certeau:

> The bridge is ambiguous everywhere: it alternatively welds together and opposes insularities. It distinguishes between them and threatens them. It liberates from enclosure and destroys autonomy. As a transgression of the limit, a disobedience of the law of the place, it represents a departure, an attack on a state, the ambition of a conquering power or the flight of an exile; in any case, the betrayal of an order. But at the same time as it offers the possibility of a bewildering exteriority, it allows or causes the re-emergence beyond the frontiers of the alien element that was controlled in the interior, and gives objectivity (that is expression and re-presentation) to the alterity that was hidden inside the limits, so that in re-crossing the bridge and

coming back within the enclosure the traveler henceforth
finds there the exteriority that he had first sought by going
outside and then fled by returning. Within the frontiers,
the alien is already there, an exoticism or sabbath of the
memory, a disquieting familiarity. It is as though delimi-
tation itself were the bridge that opens the inside to the
other.[72]

The bridge, in this depiction, is not unidirectional; travelers
move back and forth across it. It permits the "betrayal of an
order" by readmitting exiles and aliens, by opening "the inside
to the other." The inside is profoundly altered by this opening
but, at the same time, elements of its prior existence remain
intact. The "exteriority" of the other remains even in its representation. There is stability and instability in this feat of
engineering. The singular linearity of historical progress is con-
founded by the fact that these insiders and outsiders have lived
very different histories, which conflict and recombine (not
always harmoniously, not always with the same temporality) in
relation to one another as the bridge is repeatedly traversed.

I think that de Certeau's notion of a bridge that is a site of
movement back and forth is a better characterization of
history—and of what the TRC was engaged with—than the linear one that they espoused and that imagined a one-way path to
a better future. The confusion and messiness of the Commission's deliberations, what Sitze has called its "incommensurable
epistemic demands," resulted from having opened the inside,
the minority white supremacist nation-state, to its majority
black others, bringing those "exiles," that "alien element," back
into the fold. To this day, their "disquieting" presence carries
with it their "exteriority," even as they are now considered to be
"inside," in the sense of being admitted "within the frontiers"
that had once excluded them. Those brought back from exile

did not entirely lose their "exteriority," and elements of the past (structures of inequality based on race, on the racialization of class) retain their "disquieting familiarity."

The clear distinction between past and present as a way to the future was impossible to establish within the practical limits imposed on the TRC. But the distinction operated nonetheless and in two contrary ways. It gave the TRC's insistence on forgiveness a strong moral claim (as a necessary bridge to the future), and—at the same time—it undermined attention to the enduring consequences of the political and economic compromises that were being made (and that the TRC had no ability to control). The end of apartheid did signal a historical event; as at Nuremberg crimes against humanity were attributed to an evil regime now declared past. But the full extent of a judgment of history (an analysis of the structural roots of the evil and of the importance of contests for power and the role of the protagonists in those contests) was not realized; in fact, it was indefinitely deferred.

3

Calling History to Account

The Movement for Reparations for Slavery in the United States

> Social democracy thought fit to assign to the working class the role of redeemer of future generations, in this way cutting the sinews of its greatest strength. The training made the working class forget both its hatred and its spirit of sacrifice, for both are nourished by the image of enslaved ancestry rather than that of liberated grandchildren.
>
> —Walter Benjamin, *Theses on the Philosophy of History*, XII

There is a long history—dating back to well before the Civil War—of the demand for reparations for slavery and the slave trade in the United States and elsewhere.[1] The demand sometimes came in the form of an itemized request for payment of an overdue obligation, as was the case in an exchange in 1865, between a plantation owner and his now-freed slave. Replying to an inquiry from the former master about his interest in returning to work, Jourdon Anderson wrote asking for a sign of good faith:

> We have concluded to test your sincerity by asking you to send us our wages for the time we served you. This will make us forget and forgive old scores, and rely on your justice and friendship in the future. I served you faithfully for thirty-two years and Mandy twenty years. At $25 a month for me, and $2 a week for Mandy our earnings would amount to $11,680. Add to this interest for the time

our wages has been kept back and deduct what you paid for our clothing and three doctor's visits to me, and pulling a tooth for Mandy, and the balance will show what we are in justice entitled to.[2]

Anderson, who was living in Ohio, sent the letter to the *New York Daily Tribune*, thus making clear the ironic intent of his writing. More was at stake than monetary payment; this was an attempt to publicly expose the continued blindness of a former slaveholder to the wrongs he had committed. It was a way of calling to account the institution of slavery itself.

Calling to account in a broad sense is what I think the reparations movement is about—account in the sense of a tally of what is owed, but also in the sense of being answerable, being held accountable. Even when represented in monetary terms, it is not only financial compensation but historical accountability—a judgment about history—that is ultimately at stake. The need for historical reckoning is enormous for a country that has neglected the role of slavery in its very creation. A growing number of historians have shown that cotton cultivation and the enslaved labor that supported it were the key to the Industrial Revolution, to the creation of financial institutions, management techniques, and global markets—all of which enabled the rise of American capitalism and its international economic ascendancy. Sven Beckert and Seth Rockman write that "American slavery is necessarily imprinted on the DNA of American capitalism."[3] Ta-Nehisi Coates, whose article from 2014 in the *Atlantic* helped reopen the conversation on reparations, adds that "racism remains, as it has been since 1776, at the heart of this country's political life."[4] The reparations movements say it is time to take account of these facts.

But how to account for wrongs so destructive, for practices that have now been condemned as "crimes against humanity," and that have taken a lasting toll on those subjected to them, and on their descendants as well? Citing a British abolitionist writing in 1787, Stephen Best and Saidiya Hartman point out that "in his account, justice is beyond the scope of the law, and redress necessarily inadequate.... How does one compensate for centuries of violence that have as their consequence the impossibility of restoring a prior existence, of giving back what was taken or repairing what was broken?"[5] The impossibility of repair was also the issue, of course, at Nuremberg and for the South African Truth and Reconciliation Commission, but in those instances the evil being addressed was taken to belong to the past. Forms of financial compensation were eventually offered to victims of the Holocaust and of apartheid; they were meant to provide historical closure for irreparable damage.[6] The slavery reparations movements are different; they are not about closure and not about victims. The juridical logic of a benevolent state taking up the cause of victims of past evil doesn't operate in these movements' demands. For one thing, the evil is not past; for another, closure for a minority population within the nation cannot easily take the form of a new sovereign state—although there have been recurring calls for a separate black nation from within some of the movements for African American emancipation. In addition, the enslaved and their descendants are represented as agents (however exploited and oppressed) demanding their due in the form not of state benevolence, but of national accountability for a persisting evil that it is their job to describe. They charge that the continuing legacy of slavery is the racism that still lies at the very heart of American democracy; that is the history that must be held to account.

The historian Aaron Carico writes that the Civil War did not close the books on the question of slavery. "The freedom entailed by abolition did not denote an account that was to be marked 'paid in full' by the state to the ex-slave in 1865, and much less did it denote an account centuries in arrears (in such arrears that it could never hope to be repaid)."[7] Reparations movement advocates point out that subsequent decades of legislative and judicial pronouncements have not come near to acquitting the debt. The nation-state has been unable to compensate those oppressed by the system; the juridical model has failed to bring justice to those who deserve it. I will argue in what follows that even as they demand some form of financial restitution, the reparations movements recognize that the full debt "could never hope to be repaid." The point is to draw attention (and sometimes funding) to an ongoing problem, but also to hold the nation to account in the form of a rewritten history— not a linear story of gradual progress, but a record of an ongoing, unfulfilled struggle to achieve justice. David Scott calls this "a moral and reparatory history," "a history of the fundamental claim that unrequited wrongs *remain* wrongs *still*, that they do not fade with the mere passage of time."[8] This form of history is more explicitly political than that usually practiced by professional historians:

> Reparatory politics . . . is a *demand* for neither equality nor fairness. It is a demand that includes the recognition that the *unforgivable* wrong of generations of enslavement has given rise to a permanent racial debt that, while it can *never* be fully discharged has necessarily to be honored *before* any common future of freedom can begin.[9]

The appeal for reparations, unlike the imposition of retribution or the call for a redeeming forgiveness, does not assume the past is past. Coates puts it clearly: "The sins of slavery did not stop with slavery. On the contrary, slavery was but the initial crime in a long tradition of crime, of plunder even, that could be traced to the present day."[10] It is the recognition of this history that renders "untenable" the progressive narrative of American democracy, putting in its place a more complicated, uneven story in which time and place have multiple valences and in which debt is a central figure. Debt as not a monetized obligation (though it is, of course, that), but something in excess, something closer to the biblical sense of the word: a type of offense requiring expiation—a sin. This resonates with German usage in which the word *schuld* denotes both debt and guilt.

Debt

The enslavement of African Americans effectively came to an end in the United States in 1863, the third year of the Civil War; Lincoln's Emancipation Proclamation declared the enslaved free in many of the Confederate states and invited those fit to do so to join the armies of the North. Slavery continued, however, in many parts of the United States, including all of the Union slave states. At the end of the war, in 1865, slavery was abolished throughout the land with passage of the Thirteenth Amendment to the Constitution. That amendment was followed by two more "Reconstruction Amendments": the Fourteenth in 1868, which grants citizenship to anyone "born or naturalized in the United States" and stipulates equal protection of the law for them; and the Fifteenth (1870), which prohibits discrimination on the basis of "race, color, or previous condition of servitude."[11] Yet these formal pronouncements, while declaring illegal the institution of slavery and discrimination based on race, did not signal the end of the oppression of black Americans. As a minority of the country's population, their fate was subsumed to other considerations, primarily the reconciliation of the opposing forces in the war. The vision of a reunified nation did not include black people as primary citizens; indeed many proponents of emancipation—Lincoln included—thought black men and women should be given their own state or sent back to Africa. (This theme of a separate black nation echoes down the century in the projects of black nationalists, who take homogeneity to be the defining trait of nations and so call for a sovereign nation of their own from which they could not be excluded. It is not the position held by reparations movements; they take it as their task to expose and undermine the white supremacy at the heart of American democracy.) After the Civil War, local and national legislation addressed the needs of white southerners first; these were the slaveholders who had lost the human capital upon which their wealth was built. The evils associated with slavery did not come to an end, but continued in new forms, debt being chief among them.

Following the period of Reconstruction, which opened a brief window of opportunity for some freed women and men to participate in government, reaction set in. W. E. B. DuBois, Eric Foner, and others have detailed the amazing accomplishments of Reconstruction, the postwar, postenslavement euphoria in which black churches and schools flourished. In as many as twelve states coalitions of white and black candidates led to biracial state legislatures.[12] But even as these developments unfolded, the reaction was strong and harsh. At the official level, gains were reversed when Andrew Johnson succeeded to the presidency after Lincoln's assassination. He overturned General Sherman's order to distribute confiscated Confederate lands to the formerly enslaved (four hundred thousand acres to forty thousand formerly enslaved—which gave rise to the expectation that newly freed laborers would be granted "forty acres and a mule") and instead gave the land to soldiers who had served the Confederate cause. Former slaveholders were compensated for their lost property, with little attention to the economic plight of their now-freed slaves. The Bankruptcy Act of 1867 allowed property owners to retain land despite financial insolvency. And crop-lien laws established terms of contract that favored planters and that enabled them to borrow against anticipated harvests—the debt incurred to be repaid by exploiting the labor of now "free" men and women. Many southern states passed laws restricting voting; this was the period, too, of the founding of the Ku Klux Klan and of violent attacks on the lives and property of the African American population. By the late 1870s what came to be known as Radical Reconstruction was over; and by the 1890s the southern states had enacted "Jim Crow" laws in the form of poll taxes and literacy and character tests; property ownership requirements were supplemented by extralegal forms of intimidation to subjugate black Americans—the violence of lynching prime among them.

Arguably, what was most damaging from a long-term perspective was the transformation of the formerly enslaved into debtors, usually as tenant farmers or sharecroppers and as customers forced to buy on credit in local stores. (In some of these stores, Carico shows, African Americans were coerced at gunpoint into setting up charge accounts!)[13] In this way, those once enslaved were trapped anew—this time in financial relationships that they could not escape and that provided a measure of economic compensation to their former owners. Carico has brilliantly theorized this indebtedness, which he calls "a metamorphosis in the value-form of the slave."[14] "Though technically exchange value was no longer engraved in black flesh as a commodity form, this value re-attached to a number of those bodies in the red ink of the merchants' ledgers—like a kind of ghost conjured by law and capital, constantly haunting the freed and compelling their labor."[15] The American dream of accumulated

wealth and generational prosperity could not be shared by these
black sharecroppers and tenant farmers. Writes Carico:

> Their and their families' lives were to be plotted not as a
> line, like an arrow, but as a circle, like a cell. The horizons
> of their expectations were the breadth of a field of cotton
> and the length of its growing season, hemmed in by the
> annual cycles of having credit furnished and having debt
> tallied, and of never having that arithmetic add up to
> another future. Here, the quagmire of debt becomes the
> inertia of history . . . and that stuckness gets limned as
> blackness. To be or to become swamped in poverty and debt
> is to be or to become black. . . . Debt, poverty, stasis—in
> America, these have been the features of a political econ-
> omy that formulates race.[16]

Carico's conclusion asserts that there has never been closure on
the evil of slavery. "As a matter of historiography," he writes,
"1865 marks an ideological cover-up that erroneously calls slavery's time of death."[17] From the perspective of those demanding
reparations, the time of slavery's death has not yet arrived; these
are the ghosts (the zombies?) haunting all subsequent American history.

Indebtedness was not relieved by progressive legislation in
subsequent eras. Even as some measure of reform was achieved,
"debt, poverty, stasis" continued to mark most African American lives. I do not want to deny the importance of reforms that
have made legal structures more susceptible to claims against
racism and thus have achieved a measure of institutional change,
some of it permanent. But the story of black lives in America is
one of progress followed by backlash. In that story the precarious economic existence of most African Americans, which is an
effect of enduring racism, persists.

The egalitarian promise of Reconstruction was withdrawn by the end of the nineteenth century. In the twentieth, New Deal measures, which addressed the impoverished "one-third of the nation," effectively excluded black people. In order to secure Southern senators' support of FDR's Social Security insurance (for the old and the unemployed), agricultural workers and domestics—jobs in which African Americans predominated—were not covered.[18] The list goes on and on. The GI Bill (1944), which supported veterans returning from World War II in areas such as education and housing, was seemingly color blind, but it did not address or seek to correct long-standing discriminatory policies of educational institutions, banks, and realtors. Similarly, government-supported housing initiatives, which enabled home ownership and so a rise into the middle class for many Americans, engaged in discriminatory practices.[19]

In *Brown v. Board of Education* (1954), the Supreme Court declared that segregation in public schools was a violation of the equal protection clauses of the Fourteenth Amendment, thereby overturning an earlier ruling in *Plessy v. Ferguson* (1896), which had permitted "separate but equal" accommodations under that same amendment.[20] Supreme Court Associate Justice Robert Jackson (he was the chief prosecutor at the Nuremberg tribunal, who maintained that state sovereignty precluded international intervention in the domestic treatment of minorities) had worried in a private memo about the impact of the decision on "social custom" and on the "fears, prides and prejudices which this Court cannot eradicate, and which even in the North are latent, and occasionally ignite where the ratio of colored population to white passes a point where the latter vaguely, and perhaps unreasonably, feel themselves insecure."[21] Jackson insisted that it was up to Congress, not the Court, to enforce the ruling and to carry out the detailed restructuring of schools it called for. His comment that "constitutions are easier amended than social customs, and even the North never fully conformed its racial practices to its professions" proved prescient (although he was persuaded to join the unanimous opinion of the Court in the end).[22] The ability of law (coming from legislators or the courts) to enact justice in its moral sense was limited. *Brown* did unleash a host of important actions to implement the ruling, including the tremendous gains of the civil rights movement in the years that followed, but it also did not—could not—address the geographic segregation, in cities especially, that even after *Brown* held school segregation in place. As Coates puts it: "For a century after emancipation, quasi-slavery haunted the South. And more than half a century after *Brown v. Board of Education*, schools throughout much of the country remain segregated."[23] The results of this segregation served to compound the poverty and indebtedness in which much of the black population finds itself still today.

The Civil Rights Acts of 1964 and the Voting Rights Act of 1965 are important landmarks in the history of antidiscrimination law in the United States. They brought the problem of discrimination to the center of American politics and provided the means for enforcement in individual and collective cases and the grounds for legal redress in the areas of public accommodation, employment, education, and voting rights. But their impact has been less thoroughgoing than anticipated—the latest example is the impact of the Supreme Court decision in 2013 ending federal oversight of voter-suppressing states, which had the effect of unleashing voter suppression in those states in 2016 and 2018.[24]

Affirmative action was a complement to the antidiscrimination legislation, aimed particularly at integrating the workforce and higher education. Arguably it has had a measure of success in higher education, increasing the numbers of so-called "diverse" students and faculty and drawing attention to the importance of heterogeneity for any educational mission—although the determined backlash to it continues to this day.[25] In the labor force, the results were more mixed. Indeed, there was a cynical calculation by President Richard Nixon when he endorsed the Philadelphia Plan in 1969 (the Plan concerned allocating jobs based on race in the construction industry). The sociologist John David Skrentny shows that, among other things, Nixon sought to undermine the Democratic Party's constituencies, aiming to split black and white workers and to pit civil rights groups against the organized labor movement, race against class. In this—only one example in a long history of the workings of racial capitalism—he was successful in the long run.[26]

If the long run is what we look at, systematic inequality continues to characterize the white/black wealth divide in the United States. A recent report from the Center for American Progress, which called for policies to address the deepening divide between white and black households, noted that the divide has only increased since the Great Recession of 2008–2009, when subprime mortgages disproportionately targeted black homeowners and black communities lost 53 percent of their wealth.[27] The introduction to the Report summarizes the reasons:

> Black households . . . have far less access to tax-advantaged forms of saving, due in part to a long history of employment discrimination and other discriminatory practices. A well-documented history of mortgage market discrimination means that blacks are significantly less likely to be homeowners than whites, which means they have less access to the savings and tax benefits that come with owning a home. Persistent labor market discrimination and segregation also force blacks into fewer and less advantageous employment opportunities than their white counterparts. Thus,

African Americans have less access to stable jobs, good wages, and retirement benefits at work.[28]

It is not surprising then that "African Americans are burdened with more costly debt."[29]

The authors don't take up the question of mass incarceration—but the fact that black men are five times more likely to be imprisoned than white men means less access to decent jobs for them and greater poverty for their families.[30] Although the Center for American Progress report found that black families are slightly less likely to owe money than their white counterparts, their "debt payments . . . were more than twice as costly." The study concludes with a group of recommendations for "intentional systematic policy choices" that echoes proposals we have heard for over a century. "Maintaining the status quo," the authors conclude, "translates into another 200 years before African Americans have the same level of wealth as their white counterparts."[31]

Accounting

I cite these instances because the theme of debt runs through the long history of demands for reparations. But it is not a debt contracted by African Americans; it is one they are owed. It is the bad debt the nation has incurred for ever having allowed them to be enslaved. If "debt, poverty, stasis" (to use Carico's terms) have come to characterize the condition of slavery's descendants, it is not a failure of their will or agency, but a consequence of enslavement and its aftermath, say those calling for reparations. African Americans are "slavery's contemporary victims," writes Randall Robinson, whose book arguing for reparations is titled *The Debt: What America Owes to Blacks*.[32] Debt, as Carico pointed out, is enslavement in another form. It is not any longer the theft of wage labor that is operative, but a tax on so-called free labor that effectively renders freedom null. The theft continues in new form.

In the view of its advocates, reparations might begin to cancel the indebtedness that traps African Americans in cycles of poverty; and, as importantly, it would acknowledge the debt owed by a nation that has yet to recognize its obligation. The double play on the notion of debt (our financial indebtedness is a result of a moral and financial debt you owe us) moves the diagnosis away from "the culture of poverty" (blaming African Americans for their poverty and purported family dysfunction) to the structures that have kept racial inequality in place. As Martha Biondi puts it, "reparations changes the discursive image of African Americans from victims to creditors and revises the dominant narrative of American social, political, and economic history."[33] The demand for restitution of lost earnings turns African Americans into creditors who are calling due the accounts; it gives them agency, not as victims, but as people rightfully claiming what they are owed. At the same time, the demands for reparations, even when sums are specified, make clear that the debt can never be fully discharged. It is impossible to close the books on slavery and its legacy. The debt is a "bad debt," in the sense given to it by Stefano Harney and Fred Moten. It is a "debt that cannot be repaid, the debt at a distance, the debt without creditor, the black debt.... Excessive debt, incalcuable debt... debt as its own principle."[34] Although in the case of reparations, there is a creditor—the heirs to the legacy of American slavery.

Well before Emancipation, ex-slaves petitioned their masters for reimbursement for unpaid wages; as in the case I cited at the beginning of this chapter, they might be able to specify the value of the labor that had been stolen from them, but money could not compensate for other losses (family members, human dignity, life itself). The black abolitionist David Walker (1829) insisted that "the greatest riches in all America have arisen from our blood and tears";[35] a generation later (1854) another black abolitionist, Martin Delany, called for a "national indemnity . . . for the unparalleled wrongs, undisguised impositions, and unmitigated oppression, which we have suffered at the hands of this American people."[36] Delany did not specify what this indemnity amounted to—he couldn't, given the wrongs he enumerated. After slavery ended white and black groups organized to demand pensions for the formerly enslaved, sometimes as a practical measure (to assure support for elderly freed women and men), but also as a statement of principle (now that enslavement was recognized as an illegal practice, those subjected to it were owed some form of restitution). Attempting to discredit the very idea that pensions were legitimate, the federal government pressed fraud charges against some of the organizers of these pension societies, and even jailed a few of them. There was an unsuccessful lawsuit (1915) by the formerly enslaved that claimed as recompense taxes the United States had levied on cotton. The court refused the claims on the grounds of the sovereign immunity of the nation; the judges referred the plaintiffs to their former masters for compensation (suggesting that it was individual "contractual" relationships and not a state-sanctioned system of enslavement that were at issue).[37] In all of these efforts the theme not of victimhood but of stolen labor predominated. Here was Sojourner Truth in 1868: "We have been a source of wealth to this republic. Our labor supplied the country with cotton, until villages and cities dotted the enterprising North for its manufacture. . . . Beneath a burning Southern sun have we toiled, in the canebrake and the rice swamp, urged on by the merciless driver's lash, earning millions of money."[38]

But how to claim some of those millions? A century after Sojourner Truth, Martin Luther King appealed for "a massive program by the government of special compensatory measures" for repayment to the "Negro [who] was, during those years, robbed of the wages of his toil."[39] Audley Moore (1963) made the generational connection, demanding "fair and just compensation for the loss of property rights in the labor of our foreparents, for which no payment of any kind has ever been made."[40] James Forman's dramatic "Black Manifesto," delivered at the Black National Economic Conference in 1969, included a long list of demands to white Christian churches and Jewish synagogues for their active participation in the enslavement of black Americans. The monetary compensation he asked for ($15 a head for every black person in the United States—he calculated there were thirty million of them and so asked for $500 million) constituted a claim as much moral as practical—$15 a head could hardly begin to erase the debt.[41] Randall Robinson called for a "virtual Marshall Plan of federal resources" to repay "white society's debt to slavery's contemporary victims."[42] "The value of slaves' labor went into others' pockets.... Where was the money? Where is the money? There is a debt here. I know of no statute of limitations either legally or morally that would extinguish it."[43] This is a debt owed that no amount of money could ever repay.

The debt, in these calls for reparations, stands as the unfinished business of slavery, a history of evil that continues despite gestures made to relegate it to the past. It is, moreover, a collective debt, not one owed to individuals. Although it is expressed in financial terms and demands recognition as such, it exceeds any sum that can be named. David Scott makes this point about the Caribbean "politics of reparations." What it seeks, he says, "is not economic aid (with its disciplining technologies and moral hubris), not help in the subservient sense of a mendicant seeking assistance, but what is *owed* . . . by former slave-trading and slave-owning nations as a matter of the justice of redress."[44]

Although there has been litigation in the United States demanding reparations, no court can finally adjudicate the sin. From this perspective, the idea that DNA will establish the rightful heirs to wages owed to those previously enslaved is a literalizing (and a minimizing) of the aims of the reparations movements.[45] It is those subjected to racism, not only the descendants of individuals who were enslaved, who are demanding redress.

In the 1960s, the moment of decolonization, another theme was added to these reparations claims—that of the debt the nation owed to Africa as well as to African Americans. This was a way of establishing a certain national (or transnational) identity, a black majority reply to the white supremacy upon which the American nation was based. When Forman issued his manifesto, he referred to American blacks as a "colonized people inside the United States, victimized by the most vicious, racist system in the world." This enabled him to make a connection between antiracist movements in the United States and African liberation movements—they were of a piece. Some of the reparations money he demanded, he said, ought to go to establish cooperative businesses not only in the United States, but also in Africa, which he referred to as "our motherland." "We are so proud of our African heritage and realize concretely that our struggle is not only to make revolution in the United States, but to protect our brothers and sisters in Africa and to help them rid themselves of racism, capitalism and imperialism by whatever means necessary, including armed struggle."[46]

Randall Robinson also emphasized Africa in his book on reparations. For Robinson, reclaiming Africa was a way of restoring African American pride. "To be made whole again, blacks need to know the land of their forebears when its civilizations were verifiably equal to any in the world."[47] They needed to know this history in order to become agents of their own history. Reclaiming the history and culture of Africa required coordination with those nations. Robinson cited a declaration on reparations from a meeting of the Organization of African Unity in 1993 that pointed to "the damage done to Africa and to the Diaspora by enslavement, colonialism and neo-colonialism."[48] The authors of the declaration state that they are "fully persuaded that the damage sustained by the African peoples is not a theory of the past but is painfully manifested from Harare to Harlem and in the damaged economies of Africa and the black world from Guinea to Guyana, from Somalia to Surinam." The declaration calls for economic reparations and cites historic precedents—German reparations to Jews, US compensation to Japanese-Americans interned during the Second World War—but it also recognizes the limits of that claim.

Cognizant of the fact that compensation for injustice *need not necessarily be paid entirely in capital transfer* but could include service to the victims or other forms of restitution and readjustment of the relationship agreeable to both parties;

Emphasizing that an admission of guilt is a necessary step to reverse this situation;

Emphatically convinced that what matters is not the guilt but the responsibility of those states whose economic evolution once depended on slave labour and colonialism and whose forebears participated either in selling and buying Africans, or in owning them, or in colonizing them;

Convinced that the pursuit of reparations by the African peoples on the continent and in the Diaspora will be a *learning experience in self-discovery and in uniting political and psychological experience*;

Calls upon the international community to *recognize that there is a unique and unprecedented moral debt* owed to the African peoples which has yet to be paid—the debt of compensation to the Africans as the most humiliated and exploited people of the last four centuries of modern history." (my emphasis added)

In this declaration, as in Forman's and Robinson's texts, the demand for reparations becomes a full-fledged analysis of the place of slavery in the organization of a world system of haves and have nots, with racism at its very core. Racism is "not a theory of the past," but a continuing disaster, a fact of present history. "This black holocaust," Robinson insisted, "produces its victims *ad infinitum*, long after the active stage of the crime has ended."[49] The system of enslavement may be confined to the past, but there has been no closure to the crimes it committed and unleashed. Repayment of the debt is long overdue; those who are owed must hold the nation to account.

Loss

A current of loss runs through this literature on reparations, and it is not just loss of the value of labor and of the material requirements for a good life. It is expressed sometimes as the loss of dignity and humanity, the loss of connection to the rich culture and history of Africa, and the (existential) loss of trust in the possibility for a better future. "I was coming to understand," writes Ta-Nehisi Coates, "that losing things, too, was part of the journey."[50] Coates refers with these words to his personal journey, but like his collection of essays, *We Were Eight Years in Power: An American Tragedy* (2017), it is meant to stand as a comment on the long history of black people in America. I think the book can be read as allegory: Coates's awakening to the history of his people and to his place in that history is the story not only of African Americans, but of America itself—a form of David Scott's "moral and reparative history." Coates tells us that large story as he recounts his own coming to full consciousness of the power, the extent, and the endurance of white supremacy in democratic America. "The Case for Reparations" is a central chapter of the book, the culmination of his journey in the course of the eight years of the Obama presidency. That essay and the others in the book (one for each year of the Obama presidency) give us rich material for thinking about how the call for reparations addresses the experience of loss, above all loss of faith in the moral promise associated with the judgment of history. It is reparative in two senses: first, it corrects the myth of American democracy with an account that represents an "other" history; and, second, it exposes the psychic, physical, and material damage incurred by those others as they repeatedly lost out on the promise held out by the myth.

The title of the book refers both to the years of the Obama presidency and to the post–Civil War period of Reconstruction. It is taken from the words of the South Carolina congressman Thomas Miller, who, in 1895, appealed to the state constitutional convention for recognition of the accomplishments of freed men and women ("we were eight years in power") that had helped reconstruct the state and "placed it upon the road to prosperity."[51] The subtitle of Coates's book refers to the unhappy outcomes of both eras; the story is of unending tragedy, recurring disappointment, the mourning of an unending loss.

Loss is Coates's unrelenting theme—promise followed by loss: The foundational promise of the Declaration of Independence contradicted by constitutional rule that counted an enslaved individual as 3/5 of a person (in the determination of the number of state representatives in the congress). The violent denial of the promise of Reconstruction. The promise of the New Deal and the GI Bill, and the exclusion of most black people from those opportunities. The promise of *Brown v. Board of Education* followed by the murder of Emmett Till. The failures of school busing and housing desegregation in city after city. The gains of the civil rights movement and the promise of affirmative action, weakened by one court decision after another. The refusal of Congress year after year even to entertain Representative John Conyers's bill (HR40, named for the unfulfilled promise of "forty acres and a mule"), first introduced in 1989, to *study* the effects of slavery on "living African Americans."[52] The unpunished murders of so many black men. And then the Obama election and Coates's initial naive belief that "it now seemed possible that white supremacy, the scourge of American history, might well be banished in my life-time. In those days I imagined racism as a tumor that could be isolated and removed from the body of America, not as a pervasive system both native and essential to that body."[53] It takes the election of Donald Trump ("The First White President") to finally and fully disillusion him.

Coates's own emergence as a writer is an effect of the Obama presidency: "the doors swung open" for black people like him.[54] It seemed possible—his portrait of Michelle Obama illustrates this wish—that black people, black culture, black history would henceforth be seen as just another branch of the pluralist American tree. "It seemed possible that our country had indeed, at long last, come to love us."[55] If the president were black, this must mean that racial difference had ended as the organizing principle of national identity. But the backlash against Obama (recounted in "The Fear of a Black President," chapter 5), the outraged reactions to any sign of his identification with other African Americans (as when he says that the murdered Trayvon Martin could have been his son), the need for him to contain his better instincts awaken Coates to the illusion of linear progress: "I had been wrong about the possibility of Barack Obama.... I might be wrong about a good deal more."[56] And it sends him on a quest for understanding, from history books—where he discovers the deep roots of American racism—to Civil War battlefields, where he learns that he lives in a country "that will never apologize for slavery, but will not stop apologizing for the Civil War."[57] Coates's insights are not new for many historians of the United States (indeed they are old news), but his discovery—his personal journey, a naive sense of discovery—is a powerful call to a larger public to learn this history with him and to share its emotional impact.

For Coates the revelations are stunning, as he recounts his own disillusionment—his willingness over and over again to believe what he calls the American story of progress—as a haunting by history. "And now the lies of the Civil War and the lies of these post-racial years began to resonate with each other, and I could now see *history, awful and undead, reaching out from the grave.*"[58] There is no possibility of mourning the horrors of slavery, of mourning the enslaved dead, because they live on as zombies or ancestral spirits in the very souls of their descendants (all black Americans); their time has not passed. This is not a wholly pessimistic state of things, as Sarah Juliet Lauro points out in her work on "Zombie Dialectics." Tracing the origin of the myth of the zombie to Haitian slave plantations, she notes that there the zombie was "a slave raised from the dead to labor, who revolts against his masters."[59] The zombie at once signifies the social death of the slave ("biologically alive, but 'socially dead'") and its living potential for rebellion (which can bring the ultimate freedom associated with a martyr's death). The zombie is the "frozen image of [these] irresolvable opposites"—death in life, life in death.[60] We might say that for Coates, too, there is something enabling about the history of the undead—it leads to his own conviction that he needs to act.[61]

But, in order to act, he needs to mourn the death of his belief in the promise of democracy. "Mourning," Freud wrote, "is regularly the reaction to the loss of a loved person, or to the loss of some abstraction which has taken the place of one, such as one's country, liberty, an ideal, and so on."[62] Grieving the loss of his belief in the inevitable triumph of the good leads Coates to a new realization: "it was slavery that allowed American democracy to exist in the first place."[63] There was nothing "accidental" about the "hypocrisy of a nation founded by slaveholders extolling a gospel of freedom."[64] For Coates there is no closure to this loss of the ideal of American democracy. In either form—slave zombies or democracy's lie uncovered—the past lives on. At best, Coates experiences that insurmountable form of grief that Freud calls melancholia, an inability to let go of the lost object(s), an identification with them that deeply (and, for Freud, negatively) affects one's sense of self.

But Coates's melancholia, if that is what it is, has a resolution that comes in the form of a demand for reparations.

> All the threads I had been working on . . . came together in "The Case for Reparations": the critique of respectability politics, the realization that history could be denied but not escaped, the understanding of the Civil War's long shadow, the attempt to discover my own voice and language and, finally the deeply held belief that white supremacy was so foundational to this country that it would not be defeated in my lifetime, my child's lifetime, or perhaps ever. There would be no happy endings, and if there were, they would spring from chance, not from any preordained logic of human morality.[65]

In other words, the inevitable forward march of history offers neither hope nor incentive to action.

What do offer inspiration, however, are examples of defiance in the history of African American life—defiance of the kind Coates associates with the "repeated acts of self-creation" of Malcolm X.[66] "If freedom has ever meant anything to me personally," he writes of Malcolm and other resisters, "it is this defiance."[67] Perhaps, too, there is here an echo of the defiance of the zombie, the rebellious figure who will not accept enslavement in any form. The call for reparations implies the need for defiance, for collective action on the part of African Americans and their allies to demand the long-overdue recognition of the sin of enslavement so as to bury once and for all the racism of which slavery was both effect and cause. Conyers's filing of HR 40 year after year can also be seen as an act of defiance in the very body of the nation that refuses to recognize that it is infected by the racist legacy of slavery.

Reparations, then, is less a literal demand for financial repayment of debt (though for some it surely also is that) than it is a defiant rereading of the history of the United States. It is a rereading that extends beyond the black experience to a condemnation of predatory capitalism that has made race a primary instrument of its rule. In this connection, Coates writes, "I have never seen a contradiction between calling for reparations and calling for a living wage, or calling for legitimate law enforcement and single-payer health care. They are related— but cannot stand in for one another. I see the fight versus sexism, racism, poverty, and even war finding their union not in synonymity but in their ultimate goal—a world more humane."[68] Here he joins an earlier call (1967) by Martin Luther King and his associates for the enactment of a "Freedom Budget" that would "abolish the scourge of poverty" for whites and blacks in the nation as a whole. And he echoes the more recent work of the Reverend William Barber, whose "Moral Mondays" movement aims to rid the entire nation of poverty, greed, militarism, and racism. The unveiling of the role of race in the economic history of the United States explodes long-standing, congratulatory progressive histories as myth. "For Americans, the hardest part of paying reparations would not be the outlay of money. It would be acknowledging that their most cherished myth was not real."[69] This acknowledgment is a form of restitution and it opens the possibility for reclaiming the lost promise of justice, the messianic hope of the judgment of history.

Here, the rereading by David Eng and his collaborators of Freud's understanding of melancholia is useful to think with. They argue that rather than a pathological state (incomplete mourning resulting in distortions of the ego and libido), melancholia's "continuous engagement with loss and its remains ... generates sites for memory and history, for the rewriting of the past as well as the reimagining of the future."[70] Dana Luciano, reading a novel by Pauline Hopkins, an African American writer at the turn of the last century, notes that in her work, "melancholia ... comes to seem less a pathology, than a realistic response to racial conditions in the U.S."[71] This ought to recall the citation from Walter Benjamin's *Theses on the Philosophy of History* that is the epigraph for this chapter. Although Benjamin was referring to the mobilization of workers, his words apply equally to the reparations movements. They are refusing to forget, indeed they are motivated by, "hatred and [a] spirit of sacrifice ... nourished by the image of enslaved ancestry."

From this perspective, we can see a larger purpose to the moral outrage in the calls for reparations. In this literature, moral outrage is a means of achieving the psychic disposition that is a condition of possibility for political mobilization. The self-hatred that is clinically associated with melancholia and that Coates addresses at several points in his book is turned outward to the structural conditions that created it. Reparations are depicted as functioning to refuse the abjection of the enslaved and their descendants, and not only by enabling them to rise out of material poverty. The movements represent the continuing refusal—over centuries—of African Americans to accept enslavement as their fate.

It is in this sense that we can read the Organization of African Unity declaration of 1993 (cited earlier): its authors were "convinced that the pursuit of reparations by the African peoples on the continent and in the Diaspora will be a learning experience in self-discovery and in uniting political and psychological experiences."[72] Robinson waxed eloquent on the restorative effects of reparations:

> Even the *making* of a well-reasoned case for restitution will do wonders for the spirit of African Americans. It will cause them at long last to understand the genesis of their dilemma by gathering, as have all other groups, all of their history—before, during, and after slavery—into one story of themselves. To hold the story fast to their breast. To make of it, over time, a sacred text. And from it, to explain themselves to themselves and to their heirs. Tall again, as they had been long, long ago.[73]

Robinson's point is that political subjectivity depends on a connection to history. Not a conventional history, I imagine, but one that uncovers hidden stories, temporalities that don't reflect the linear national model. Beyond empowering black Americans, Robinson wrote, a history that acknowledged crimes present and past would benefit all Americans. "We could disinter a buried history," Robinson wrote, "connect it to another, more recent and mistold, and give it as a healing to the whole of our people, to the whole of America."[74] These reparative histories, reclaiming what has been stolen, buried, and long denied, would not only announce but also enable an outlet for melancholia by understanding it not as individual pathology but as a historical condition: as Luciano puts it, "the very condition, indeed, of being historical."[75] For Coates the stakes are high: "What I'm talking about is a national reckoning that would lead to spiritual renewal. . . . Reparations would mean a revolution of the American consciousness, a reconciling of our self-image as the great democratizer with the facts of our history."[76]

The "facts of our history," revealed in the case for reparations, will—it is hoped—bring into being a judgment of history. It is in this sense that Coates turns to the Yale president and Congregational minister Timothy Dwight to make the case for reparations. Writing in 1810, Dwight condemned the institution of slavery and insisted that his generation hold themselves responsible for it. "It is in vain to alledge, that *our ancestors* brought them hither, and not we." "We inherit our ample patrimony with all its encumbrances; and are bound to pay the debts of our ancestors. *This* debt, particularly, we are bound to discharge: and, when the righteous Judge of the Universe comes to reckon with his servants, he will rigidly exact the payment at our hands."[77] Coates, writing some two hundred years later, is still awaiting the final judgment that will exorcise the hold of the evil of racism on the American nation, sending the undead to their eternal rest. But in the meantime, the melancholy attached to the contemplation of that experience becomes a motivation for collective political action.

The righteous Judge of the Universe is, in our secular age, understood to be History itself. But, I would argue, it is not History, conceived as an autonomous movement whose infallible judgment will right all wrongs, that is wanted. What is called for is a humanly written account that unflinchingly takes cognizance of "the facts of our history," exposing their structural and ideological supports and their varying and conflicting temporalities. It is never a question, in these movements, of an alternative to the nation; the point is that minorities have a claim on citizenship and on the founding principles as well as the treasured story of the Republic.

Facing "the facts of our history," the reparations movements insist, will force the nation to recognize a debt that can never be repaid. Paradoxically, the acknowledgment of the impossibility of repayment calls upon us to imagine the creation of more just futures. The recognition of that impossibility is an opening to possibility. And it is reparatory, not only psychically but politically as well. This, I suggest, is the ultimate import of the reparations movements: they call history (defined as human action, past, present, and future) to account. David Scott's characterization is apt in this regard: "Reparatory justice responds . . . to a *retemporalization* of history; it attunes itself to a *reenchanted* past understood as a time not yet past that continues to disfigure the present and foreclose the future."[78]

There is some evidence that the movements' call to rewrite history has gone beyond the work of some critical historians (who have long been doing just that) to the popular/public realm. On August 20, 2019, the *New York Times Magazine* devoted a special issue to "1619." In it the editors argued that the real beginning of America was not 1776, but 1619, when chattel slaves first arrived in the land. "This is sometimes referred to as the country's original sin, but it is more than that: it is the country's very origin." The goal of the 1619 project, they said, was to reframe American history, with slavery at its core. "By acknowledging this shameful history . . . perhaps we can prepare ourselves for a more just future."[79] The "perhaps" is important in that sentence; it holds out no guarantee, no utopian plan, just a wish that history retold might inaugurate change.

Epilogue

Revisioning History

It is because redemption is impossible that there is a demand for justice and an imperative of justice.... Judgment Day is both concrete (particular, political, historical) and doomed to remain historically, eternally, deferred.
    —Shoshana Felman, *The Juridical Unconscious*

I began the research that has become this book by expressing my amazement in the wake of the Charlottesville demonstrations that "the things we are experiencing"—proud identification with Nazis and Klansmen—were "still possible" in the twenty-first century. Even as I understood as naive and fantastic my expectation that the "judgment of history" would have long ago ruled these things out of order, I somehow held to the idea that it should have been possible. And, as the examples I cited in the preface indicate, I was not alone in this belief. There seems to be an abiding faith (at least for the general public and for some professional historians) that "in the end" we will be vindicated by History. The notion of history this evokes is multiple: it is at once the universal (and progressive) direction of life, the human actions that take place in unilinear time and whose Truth will eventually be recognized, and the record compiled of those actions by historians.

Although judgment implies interpretation, indeed the possibility of more than one interpretation, there is a certain finality assumed for the judgment of history. The case is closed, the guilty condemned, the innocents vindicated—this is the consoling fantasy we have inherited from the Enlightenment. That it is no longer, indeed never was, tenable has been the argument of this book. This does not mean that appeals to history's judgment, along with actual attempts to enact it, do not exist. They do. They rest on a notion of temporality that dates to the eighteenth century: a single line of change that divides time neatly into past, present, and future; traditional (or primitive) and modern; superstitious (religious) and secular. And they take the nation-state to be the "tip of the arrow" of the direction of history. This idea of history, I have tried to show, constitutes a politics that needs to interrogated. That is a politics in which the seeming resolution of moral questions (the assignment of some evil to the past, the certainty that truth will prevail in the future) over-shadows or denies persisting structures of power—structures of power that are, in effect, naturalized as the inevitable products of the necessary telos of history. The focus on the nation-state as the telos of history (and so the ultimate source of justice) also obscures the conflicts that challenge and change those struc-tures of power. It renders invisible dissenting agencies that pro-vide alternative visions of how life might be lived together.

At Nuremberg, I argued, the racism that Hannah Arendt associated with nationalism and imperialism was obscured by exclusive attention to aberrant Nazi crimes against humanity. The judgment of history that assigned Nazism to the barbaric, uncivilized past represented the victorious nation-states as avatars of the progress of history, even as their treatment of domestic minorities and colonial subjects went unremarked. The trial was meant to affirm the international covenants upon which rested the future of their status as individual sovereign nation-states. History's judgment was said to lie in the hands of the victorious nation-states, which meted out retribution in the name of the victims of National Socialism. In South Africa, the

Truth and Reconciliation Commission, unable in the context of a negotiated settlement to achieve the kind of closure the Nuremberg judges imposed, brought to light in the testimony of witnesses the truth of apartheid's brutality. Indeed, the word *truth* in the Commission's title was meant to be the synonym for history and thus the basis for a judgment of history. But there, the call to the victims of white minority rule to forgive their oppressors—in the name of a higher morality—foreclosed an analysis (demanded by some critics of the TRC) of the structures of racial capitalism, and the alternatives posed by dissidents to those structures, on which the system of domination had been based. The quasi-judicial status of the TRC established the state as the arbiter of truth and justice; in the process it was as victims rather than as resisters that those oppressed by the system came to be defined. I would say that the moral judgment—that apartheid was an evil system rightly relegated to the dustbin of history—prevailed, but that the judgment about what had enabled and challenged its power relations was occluded. The emphasis on moral closure drew attention away from the structural bases for white supremacy; despite the electoral enfranchisement of the black majority, the egalitarian future imagined by the nation's freedom fighters has yet to be realized.

In both cases—at the Nuremberg Tribunal and for the TRC—the belief that the nation was the agent of history's judgment went unquestioned, although, of course, in South Africa, the aim was to produce a nonracial "heterotopia of rich diversity," not a "stifling homogeneous nation." Still although the constitution enshrined gender equality as one of the foundational principles of the new nation, it has yet to be realized in the hierarchies of politics. In addition, the success of this nonracialist vision has lately been called into question by xenophobic attacks on black non-South Africans in disputes over the status of migrant laborers from outside the country.[1] The citizens of South Africa may be black and white, but an exclusionary politics nonetheless has been mobilized in the name of the homogeneity of national identity.

The movements for reparations for slavery in the United States present a different, critical perspective, one that acknowledges the failure of successive judgments of history to address the nation's "original sin" of slavery. In this example, it's not so much judgment that's called for—in the sense of a ruling that will consign evil to the past. Rather, it's precisely an accounting, a demand for the recognition that the past has not passed, that progressive linear narratives are untenable because they misrepresent American history. The nation as the unit of history remains unquestioned, but the conception of that history is radically revised. This is a demand not only for a different history, but, in Benjamin's sense, for "a different view of history." It is a view that abjures history's redemptive function, instead taking history to be a record of discontinuity and multiple temporalities (the lived times of the enslaved and their descendants are different from those of white Americans), a process of contention and conflict, a story of struggles with and for power, with no sharp boundaries between past, present, and future.

My reading of the reparations movements as calling for a different view of history is made possible by ongoing discussions among philosophers, political theorists, and historians about the impact of the end of the master narratives of modernity. For even as appeals to the judgment of history continue to mark public discourse, they function more as consolatory polemic in the present than as evidence of deep confidence in the future. Our condition of postmodernity, as Wendy Brown has described it, is marked by "the loss of historical direction, and with it the loss of futurity characteristic of the late modern age."[2] "We know ourselves to be saturated by history, we feel the extraordinary force of its determinations; we are also steeped in a discourse of its insignificance, and, above all, we know that history will no longer (always already did not) act as our redeemer."[3]

For Brown, as for many other commentators, the question is about what this "loss of futurity" portends for politics, what substitute visions are possible to nurture the desire for progressive change. The answers vary: Brown, seeking an alternative to the resentment-driven identity politics of the 1990s (which have returned with even greater intensity in our twenty-first century), suggests that the individualizing, essentializing language of "I am" be supplanted with the language of "I want this for us." By substituting the language of collective wanting for the language of individual being, she writes, the common good could become the object of political desire, thus "forging an alternative future."[4] Jacques Derrida, looking to reclaim something of a Marxist spirit to counter the conservative publicist Francis Fukuyama's declaration of the end of history, refuses to relinquish "a certain experience of the emancipatory promise, . . . a messianism without religion, even a messianic without messianism, an idea of justice—which we distinguish from law or right or even human rights—and an idea of democracy—which we distinguish from its current concept and from its determined predicates today."[5] The key for Derrida is the notion of promise, "as *promise* and not as onto-theological or teleo-eschatological program or design. Not only must one not renounce the emancipatory desire, it is necessary to insist on it more than ever . . . and insist on it, moreover, as the very indestructibility of the 'it is necessary.' This is the condition of a re-politicization, perhaps of another concept of the political."[6] Fredric Jameson finds in utopian imaginings a disruption of the notion that "there is no alternative to the system"; utopias serve to negate the sense of immutability in the present and so enable our "ability to imagine a different future."[7] Gary Wilder finds in the Frankfurt

School (Adorno, Benjamin) an alternative to the old idea of history as progress because, as he puts it, "relations of domination are mediated by the idea and the reality of progress itself." The concept of "anticipation" is his analytic proposal: "a kind of political disposition whereby radical actors cultivate a state of readiness for any possibility at every possible moment." This, combined with "a positive vision of what a better society might look like," sets the stage for action when the moment arrives or seems right. Wilder recognizes that anticipation involves maintaining "a balancing act between identifying concrete possibilities through utopian imagination while not foreclosing outcomes through predictive naming." It's a tricky balance to maintain. And he deems anticipation a dialectical conception: it is "a *calling for* that is also a *calling forth*, an enacted idea that may bring into being what it desires through the performance itself (even as that very image of future possibilities only arises through such performative acts)."[8] Mark Fisher says that "politicization requires a political agent who can transform the taken for granted into the up-for-grabs."[9] It's precisely the up-for-grabs (no telos, no predictive naming) that anticipates the future for the present in ways we cannot prefigure. In a similar vein, Michael Löwy writes of history as an "open process, not determined in advance, in which surprises, unexpected strokes of good fortune and unforeseen opportunities may appear at any moment." We need to be prepared, he continues, "to grasp the fleeting moment in which revolutionary action is possible."[10]

Despite important differences among these writers (and I have chosen only a few of the many writing on these topics), they share the notion that it is possible to think the future without the telos of history. One doesn't have to know what the end will look like in order to seek to change the present; political desire can be provoked by utopias, driven by collective desire, enthralled by the messianic promise of an abstraction called justice, or expressed in terms of the anticipation of possibility, but it never follows predestined routes.

In fact, thinking (desiring, anticipating) the promise of the future may not always be the initial incentive to action, although the action taken itself may lead to change. Here it is useful to remember some of Michel Foucault's writings. Foucault thought that resistance and refusal did not come from outside, but were built in to relations of power; they did not depend on a vision of an alternative future as much as on a refusal of present conditions of rule, usually in the name of prior principles for organizing life together. The rise of governmentality (and, with it, *raison d'état*), he wrote, produced not only obedient subjects, but insubordinate ones, those who objected to being governed "like that."

> I do not mean that governmentalization would be opposed, in a kind of face-off by the opposite affirmation 'we do not want to be governed and we do not want to be governed at all.' I mean that, in this great preoccupation about the way to govern, . . . we identify a perpetual question which would be: how not to be governed *like that*, by that, in the name of those principles, with such and such an objective in mind and by means of such procedures, not like that, not for that, not by them.[11]

"Not to want to be governed like that also means not wanting to accept these laws because they are unjust because . . . they hide a fundamental illegitimacy."[12] These refusals are articulated in the name of different legal regimes: a communally based system of justice that is the antithesis of proprietary capitalist individualism, refusals that seek to hold on to some set of present practices against the seemingly relentless tides of change. As I noted in chapter 3, Ta-Nehisi Coates says he is inspired by the defiance of African Americans like Malcolm

X—defiance is another form of refusal.[13] So was the unwilling-ness to forgive (cited in chapter 2), expressed by some of the witnesses before South Africa's Truth and Reconciliation Commission.

Massimiliano Tomba takes some of these observations to their radical conclusion as he reconceptualizes history and poli-tics. In his work on *Insurgent Universality*, and more recently on the concept and political practice of sanctuary, he refuses moder-nity's singular time line, suggesting that certain past practices of refusal constitute "arsenal[s] of possibility" for contemporary "innovative political action."[14] If they are to be considered anachronisms because they harken back to some past, he says, they nonetheless have contemporary political uses, reminding us that the reason of state is an instrument of power, not a fact of nature, that what Foucault referred to as "illegalisms" were only so because they defied the state's definition of law and jus-tice. Tomba's insurgents refuse the domination inherent in the statist/capitalist relationships of modern nation-states; they rely on other authorities to offer alternatives to the oppression they experience. At many moments in the past, particularly moments of crisis (when things were up for grabs), alternative legal regimes have been invoked, different standards of what counted as jus-tice insisted upon. "Those who *disobey* the legal regime of mod-ern property relations do so not simply against it, but because they *obey* a different order of duties and rights based on differ-ent customs and traditions."[15] When we discard the "unilinear conception of history that culminates in European modernity," he writes, "the Middle Ages do not find a necessary outcome in capitalist and state modernity, but appear as an arsenal of pos-sibilities, a clump of roads not taken and historical layers that continue to run alongside the dominant trajectory of Western modernity."[16] In other words, there are multiple temporali-ties whose time is not exhausted, whose possibilities are not

foreclosed by their (politically motivated and arbitrary) assignment to "the past."

This kind of thinking about politics—the exploration of
alternatives to the judgment of history—has important reso-
nances for historians, those of us charged with making sense for
the present of the past. In this view, there is no guarantee that
progress is the necessary condition (direction) of life, but there
is evidence to be found in the archive of human endeavor that
actions taken can bring about change, that there have been
things worth fighting for even if success was not assured, that
the refusal and resistance to domination are motivated as much
by ethical notions of justice as by hope, and that messianic prom-
ises may offer inspiration but no reliable roadmap to the future.

In this book, I have not for the most part (in the chapters on
the Nuremberg Tribunal and the TRC) provided histories of
these "illegalisms," of alternative routes to the main highway of
modernity that "continue to run alongside" it. My focus has been
on the ways in which invocations of the judgment of history have
provided simple moral justifications for complex political matters, and have assumed the nation-state (the telos of history) to
be the ultimate source for rectifying the suffering of victims of
injustice. In so doing, this vision of history occluded the vital
role played by those who "refuse to be governed like that," and
whose self-definition has been not as victims, but as judges
themselves. The appeal to the judgment of history does not have
to operate only as a consoling fantasy, seemingly deferring action
to a force (History) outside our control.

The chapter on the reparation movements provides a different usage, a counterexample, one in which the demand for a
judgment of history is a demand for accountability in the form of
a radically reconceived history of the United States. The movements recall and enact the agency of their forebears, exposing
the "bad debt" (the original sin) at the heart of the American

nation. If it rests on a belief that progress is possible, it also refuses the idea that the juridical processes of the state can ensure that progress.

When I gave these lectures at Columbia University, my interlocutors pressed me for my own vision of history. If there is no guarantee of a better future, they asked, what view of history can we/do you work with? My answer is that we can depend neither on an autonomous redemptive force (History) nor on the ultimate good sense of some putative universal human reason to implement regimes of equality and justice. I cited Shoshana Felman as the epigraph for this chapter because, like her, I believe that Judgment Day, in the sense of a final reckoning, is "doomed to remain eternally, historically deferred." It is precisely the impossibility of its realization that moves us to action nonetheless. That action is inspired by ethical principles (forged in time) and by history's evidence of refusals (defiance) to accept the rule of the powerful, evidence of human actors proposing alternative roads to travel. With these we can think history differently, as plural modes of being whose relationships we inhabit, at least in part as a consequence of the actions that we take. Walter Benjamin, writing of the "professional conspirator . . . Blanqui," insisted that his activities "certainly do not presuppose any belief in progress—they merely presuppose a determination to do away the present injustice."[17] It is not the fear or promise of history's ultimate judgment that moves us, but the sense that—in the face of what we deem to be injustice—we have no other choice.

ACKNOWLEDGMENTS

The occasion of the Ruth Benedict Lectures was a chance to clarify and expand my thinking on the questions raised in this book. I had explored some of the ideas earlier, in the Natalie Zemon Davis lectures at the Central European University (subsequently published as a book), but I knew I needed to think harder about some of the issues I had raised. The group that assembled at Columbia in the spring of 2019 was the ideal forum for me. A core of friends and colleagues attended all three lectures, enabling the conversations to deepen, the limits and possibilities of my arguments to be revealed. Some even followed up with long, thoughtful emails, pushing me to think along lines I hadn't before considered.

For their generous and rigorous questioning, I thank David Scott, Gary Wilder, Judith Surkis, Mischa Suter, Grace Davie, Rosalind Morris, Mara de Gennaro, Nadia Abu El Haj, Joseph Massad, Gil Anidjar, Maggie Hennefeld, Zahid Chaudhary, Hannah Chazin, Alexa Stiller, Jim Dingeman, Claudio Lomnitz, and Michael Levine. Conversations with Gayle Salomon and Robert Post were most helpful. Early versions of the lectures were read by Brian Connolly, Andrew Zimmerman,

Andreas Ekert, David Bond, Daniel Aldana Cohen, and Adam Ashforth, all of whom provided leads to more reading and suggestions for rethinking some of my assertions. Max Tomba read the manuscript just before I submitted it and prodded me to make more explicit my thinking about justice and the nation-state. Jennifer Crewe has been a supportive and encouraging editor. My experience with these lectures confirmed for me an insight I've long had about academic work: the production of critical knowledge is a collective enterprise, it takes a seminar (or a series of them) to expand the thinking of any lone individual.

NOTES

Preface

1. www.marxists.org/history/cuba/archive/castro/1953/10/16.htm. Thanks to Julie Skurski for reminding me of this.
2. Telford Taylor, *Nuremberg and Vietnam: An American Tragedy* (Chicago: Quadrangle, 1970), 184.
3. www.researchgate.net/post/The_arc_of_the_moral_universe_is_long_but_it_bends_toward_justice.
4. Michael Luo, "American's Exclusionary Past and Present and the Judgment of History," *New Yorker*, August 17, 2019.
5. John Lewis comment cited by Timothy Egan, "The Smoking Gun Is Trump Himself," *New York Times*, September 28, 2019.
6. "Citizen Comey Is Fretting Over Vote: I Feel Stuck," *New York Times*, October 12, 2019.
7. Susana Narotzky, " 'A Cargo del Futuro' Between History and Memory: An Account of the 'Fratricidal' Conflict During Revolution and War in Spain (1936–39)," *Critique of Anthropology* 27, no. 4 (2007): 425.
8. Heinrich Regius [Max Horkheimer], *Dawn and Decline*, cited in Michael Löwy, *Fire Alarm: Reading Walter Benjamin's "On the Concept of History,"* trans. Chris Turner (London: Verso, 2016), 32.

9. Although there isn't much explicitly about gender in the pages that follow, analyses of constructions of difference play a big part in my reading of the materials I've worked with. And, to the extent that the question of the modern state and its relationship to history is at the center of my concern, I'm dealing with an institution whose implicit masculinity is assumed, albeit in different ways in the cases I study.

10. Georg Wilhelm Friedrich Hegel, *Philosophy of Right*, trans. T. M. Knox (Oxford: Clarendon, 1952), §340.

11. Cited in Reinhart Koselleck, *Futures Past: On the Semantics of Historical Time*, trans. Keith Tribe (New York: Columbia University Press, 2004), 38.

12. Koselleck, 33.

13. Koselleck, 103, 106.

14. Walter Benjamin, *Theses on the Philosophy of History*, XIII, in Benjamin, *Illuminations*, trans. Harry Zohn (New York: Schocken, 1968), 261.

15. Koselleck, *Futures Past*, 199.

16. Michel de Certeau, *The History of Writing*, trans. Tom Conley (New York: Columbia University Press, 1999), 41.

17. Immanuel Kant, "Idea of a Universal History from a Cosmopolitan Point of View," in *Essays and Treatises on Moral, Political, and Various Philosophical Subjects*, vol. 1 (London: William Richardson, 1798), 412–13.

18. Michel Foucault, *The Order of Things: An Archaeology of the Human Sciences* (New York: Vintage, 1994), 219. See also Ed Cohen, "A 'Special' Difference: For a Foucauldian/Feminist Genealogy of Freud," *History of the Present* 9, no. 1 (2019): 1–26.

19. Koselleck, *Futures Past*, 40–41.

20. Koselleck, 198.

21. Massimiliano Tomba, *Insurgent Universality: An Alternative Legacy of Modernity* (New York: Oxford University Press, 2019), 3.

22. Massimiliano Tomba, *Marx's Temporalities*, trans. Peter D. Thomas and Sara R. Farris (Chicago: Haymarket, 2013), 168.

23. Koselleck, *Futures Past*, 16.

24. Carl Schmitt, *The Nomos of the Earth*, trans. G. L. Ulmen (Candor, NY: Telos, 2006), 149.

25. Schmitt, 131.

26. Michel Foucault, *Security, Territory, Population: Lectures at the Collège de France, 1977–78*, trans. Graham Burchell (New York: Picador, 2007), 266–67.

27. Foucault, 259.

28. Foucault, 259.

29. Schmitt, *Nomos*, 127.

30. Joan Wallach Scott, *Sex and Secularism* (Princeton: Princeton University Press, 2018).

31. Gary Wilder, *Freedom Time: Negritude, Decolonization, and the Future of the World* (Durham, NC: Duke University Press, 2015).

32. Nicola Perugini and Neve Gordon, *The Human Right to Dominate* (Oxford: Oxford University Press, 2015), 30.

33. Judith Butler, *Frames of War: When Is Life Grievable?* (London: Verso, 2009), 134–35.

34. Samera Esmeir, *Juridical Humanity: A Colonial History* (Stanford: Stanford University Press, 2012).

35. Hannah Arendt, *The Origins of Totalitarianism* (New York: Harcourt Brace, 1966), 230.

36. Arendt, 184.

37. Cited in Adam Ashforth, *Witchcraft: Violence and Democracy in South Africa* (Chicago: University of Chicago Press, 2005), 365.

38. Randall Robinson, *The Debt: What America Owes to Blacks* (New York: Penguin, 2001), 33, 216.

1. The Nation-State as the Telos of History

1. Robert H. Jackson, *The Case Against the Nazi War Criminals: Opening Statement for the United States of America* (New York: Knopf, 1946), 7.

2. Shoshana Felman, *The Juridical Unconscious: Trials and Traumas in the Twentieth Century* (Cambridge, MA: Harvard University Press, 2002), 11.

3. Felman, 15.

4. Jackson, *The Case Against the Nazi War Criminals*, 7.

5. Cited in Michael R. Marrus, *The Nuremberg War Crimes Trial, 1945–46: A Documentary History* (Boston: Bedford, 1997), 43.

6. Jackson, *The Case Against the Nazi War Criminals*, vi.

7. Jackson, 82.

8. On this, see the work of Tim Mason, "National Socialism and the German Working Class, 1925–May 1933," *New German Critique* 5, no. 11 (1977): 49–93; and Mason, "Worker's Opposition in Nazi Germany," *History Workshop Journal* 2 (1981): 120–37.

9. Cited in Elizabeth Borgwardt, *A New Deal for the World: America's Vision for Human Rights* (Cambridge MA: Harvard University Press, 2005), 242.

10. Borgwardt, 242.

11. Jackson, *The Case Against the Nazi War Criminals*, 13.

12. Jackson, 47.

13. Cited in Marrus, *The Nuremberg War Crimes Trial*, 45.

14. Marrus, 33.

15. Borgwardt, *A New Deal for the World*, 229–30. She cites Mississippi Senator John Rankin, who saw exactly the dangers of the precedent Jackson was hoping to avoid: "If we people of the Southern States had been treated in the same manner after the War between the States as those people [the Germans] have been treated under pressure of a certain racial minority, you would not have heard the last of it until doomsday." He went on to urge that the United States "treat the people of Germany . . . with humanity and decency and . . . not permit racial minorities to vent their sadistic vengeance upon them" (233–34).

16. Alexa Stiller, "The Mass Murder of the European Jews and the Concept of 'Genocide' in the Nuremberg Trials: Reassessing Raphael Lemkin's Impact," *Genocide Studies and Prevention: An International Journal* 13, no. 1 (2019): 167.

17. James Q. Whitman, *Hitler's American Model: The United States and the Making of Nazi Race Law* (Princeton: Princeton University Press, 2017), 77.

18. Whitman, 9.

19. Whitman, 145.

20. Whitney Harris, *Tyranny on Trial* (Dallas: Southern Methodist University Press, 1999), 511.

21. François de Menthon, "Opening Address" (January 17, 1946), in Marrus, *The Nuremberg War Crimes Trial*, 91–92.

22. de Menthon, 92.

23. Jackson, *The Case Against the Nazi War Criminals*, 119.

24. Jackson, 119.

25. Jackson, 48.

26. Cited in Borgwardt, *A New Deal for the World*, 229.

27. Léon Poliakov, *Harvest of Hate: The Nazi Program for the Destruction of the Jews of Europe* (1951; New York: Holocaust Library, 1986), 263–64, cited in Stiller, "The Mass Murder of the European Jews," 166.

28. Stiller, "The Mass Murder of the European Jews," 160.

29. Jackson, *The Case Against the Nazi War Criminals*, 47.

30. Robert Meister, *After Evil: A Politics of Human Rights* (New York: Columbia University Press, 2011), 40.

31. Meister, 131–33.

32. Jackson, *The Case Against the Nazi War Criminals*, 78.

33. Jackson, 76.

34. Cited in Borgwardt, *A New Deal for the World*, 213.

35. Carl Schmitt, *The Nomos of the Earth*, trans. G. L. Ulmen (New York: Telos, 2006), 149.

36. Menthon, "Opening Address."

37. A. J. P. Taylor, *The Origins of the Second World War* (New York: Atheneum, 1962), 13.

38. Walter Ulbricht, the future leader of the German Democratic Republic, had put it in these terms well before the Tribunal. "The tragedy of the German people consists in the fact that they obeyed a band of criminals. . . . The German working class and the productive parts of the population failed before history." Cited in Tony Judt, *Postwar: A History of Europe Since 1945* (New York: Penguin 2005), 59.

39. Jackson, *The Case Against the Nazi War Criminals*, 16–17.

40. Schmitt, *Nomos*, 199.

41. "And here we have to see—as Adorno cautioned us—that violence in the name of civilization reveals its own barbarism, even as it 'justifies' its own violence by presuming the barbaric subhumanity of the other against whom that violence is waged." Judith Butler, *Frames of War: When Is Life Grievable?* (London: Verso, 2009), 93.

42. Jackson, *The Case Against the Nazi War Criminals*, 81.

43. Jackson, 88–89.

44. Cited in Borgwardt, *A New Deal for the World*, 207.

45. Jackson, *The Case Against the Nazi War Criminals*, 29.

46. Menthon, "Opening Address," 91–93.

47. Harris, *Tyranny on Trial*, xx.

48. Jackson, *The Case Against the Nazi War Criminals*, 17, 6.

49. Jackson, 59.

50. William Shirer, *The Rise and Fall of the Third Reich: A History of Nazi Germany* (New York: Simon and Schuster, 1960), 1080.

51. Cited in David Blackbourn and Geoff Eley, *The Peculiarities of German History: Bourgeois Society and Politics in Nineteenth Century Germany* (Oxford: Oxford University Press, 1984), 73. Blackbourn and Eley offer a compelling critique of the *Sonderweg* in this book.

52. Hannah Arendt, *The Origins of Totalitarianism* (New York: Harcourt, Brace, 1973), 165–66. For an extended discussion of these issues, see Judith Butler, *Parting Ways: Jewishness and the Critique of Zionism* (New York: Columbia University Press, 2012).

53. Theodor W. Adorno, *Critical Models: Interventions and Catchwords*, trans. Henry W. Pickford (New York: Columbia University Press, 1998), 89.

54. Arendt, *Origins*, 290.

55. Nicola Perugini and Neve Gordon, *The Human Right to Dominate* (Oxford: Oxford University Press, 2015), 20.

56. Perugini and Gordon, 36. See Arendt, *Eichmann in Jerusalem: A Report on the Banality of Evil* (New York: Penguin, 1983) on the question of Israel's jurisdiction for crimes committed before it became a nation. See also Adam Shatz: "After the Eichmann trial the Holocaust would increasingly supply the state with a

narrative to justify its policies, especially vis-à-vis the 'Arab Nazis.' In effect, the Jewish state would 'Israelise' the Holocaust, much as it would conquer and 'Judaise' the land." Shatz, "We Are Conquerors," *London Review of Books* 41, no. 20 (2019), www.lrb.co .uk/v41/n20/adam-shatz/we-are-conquerors.

57. Perugini and Gordon, *The Human Right to Dominate*, 37.

58. Meister, *After Evil*, 131–33. See also Butler, *Parting Ways*, on critics of this form of nationhood.

59. Wendy Brown, *Walled States, Waning Sovereignties* (New York: Zone, 2010), 71.

2. The Limits of Forgiveness

1. Some forty thousand people died in political violence in this period, more than in the entire period of the TRC's mandate (from 1960 on). Adam Ashforth, *Witchcraft, Violence, and Democracy in South Africa* (Chicago: University of Chicago Press, 2005), 276.

2. See the moving account in the novel by Nadine Gordimer, *None to Accompany Me* (New York: Farrar, Straus, and Giroux, 1994), 241. "With his assassination the meaning of the position of the young leader in negotiations becomes clearer than it has ever been; his presence carried the peculiar authority of the guerrilla past in working for peace. If men like him wanted it, who could doubt that it was attainable? If a man like him was there to convince his young followers, could they fail to listen to him?"

3. These acts were overturned in 1995, but the protection from prosecution of former agents of the apartheid state remained in effect. Adam Sitze, *The Impossible Machine: A Genealogy of South Africa's Truth and Reconciliation Commission* (Ann Arbor: University of Michigan Press, 2013), 26–27.

4. Desmond Mpilo Tutu, *No Future Without Forgiveness* (New York: Doubleday, 1999), 21.

5. Tutu, 20.

6. Jacques Derrida, *On Cosmopolitanism and Forgiveness*, trans. Mark Dooley and Michael Hughes (London: Routledge, 2001), 43.

7. Derrida, 39.

8. Derrida, 43.

9. Derrida, 45.

10. Sitze, *The Impossible Machine*, 193–200.

11. Peter Thomas, "Historical-Critical Dictionary of Marxism: Catharsis," *Historical Materialism* 17 (2009): 263.

12. Kader Asmal, Louise Asmal, and Ronald Suresh Roberts, *Reconciliation Through Truth: A Reckoning of Apartheid's Criminal Governance* (Cape Town: David Philip, 1997), 208.

13. Asmal, Asmal, and Roberts, 49.

14. Asmal, Asmal, and Roberts, 47.

15. Asmal, Asmal, and Roberts, 11.

16. Asmal, Asmal, and Roberts, 214.

17. Asmal, Asmal, and Roberts, 48.

18. Asmal, Asmal, and Roberts, 214.

19. Asmal, Asmal, and Roberts, 9.

20. Desmond Mpilo Tutu, foreword to *To Remember and to Heal*, ed. H. Russel Botman and Robin M. Peterson (Cape Town: Human and Rousseau, 1996), 7–8.

21. Derrida, *On Cosmopolitanism and Forgiveness*, 43.

22. Tutu, *No Future Without Forgiveness*, 279.

23. D. M. Davis, "The South African Truth Commission and the AZAPO Case: A Reflection Almost Two Decades Later," in *Anti-Impunity and the Human Rights Agenda*, ed. Karen Engle, Zinaida Miller, and D. M. Davis (Cambridge: Cambridge University Press, 2016), 129.

24. Alejandro Castillejo-Cuéllar, "Knowledge, Experience, and South Africa's Scenarios of Forgiveness," *Radical History Review* 97 (2007).

25. Tutu, *No Future Without Forgiveness*, 279.

26. Tutu, "Speech: No Future Without Forgiveness (Version 2)," 2003, Archbishop Desmond Tutu Collection Textual 15, https://digitalcommons.unf.edu/archbishoptutupapers/15.

27. Cited in Jill Staufer, *Ethical Loneliness: The Injustice of Not Being Heard* (New York: Columbia University Press, 2015), 121.

28. Truth and Reconciliation Commission of South Africa (TRC), *Truth and Reconciliation Commission of South Africa Report* (1998–99), 7 vols., Johannesburg. See also Truth and Reconciliation Commission of South Africa, www.justice.gov.za/trc/report/index.htm, 1:133.

29. Asmal, Asmal, and Roberts, *Reconciliation Through Truth*, 165–66.

30. Truth and Reconciliation Commission Report, 1:133.

31. Truth and Reconciliation Commission Report, 5:11.

32. Truth and Reconciliation Commission Report, 1:134.

33. Greg Grandin, "The Instruction of the Great Catastrophe: Truth Commissions, National History, and State Formation in Argentina, Chile, and Guatemala," *American Historical Review* (2005): 48.

34. Tutu, *No Future Without Forgiveness*, 212. Much to the distress of the Commission, the ANC also demanded that the culpability of its members for crimes against humanity be deleted from the report.

35. de Klerk cited in Asmal, Asmal, and Roberts, *Reconciliation Through Truth*, 213–14.

36. Truth and Reconciliation Commission Report, 5:436.

37. Ashforth, *Witchcraft, Violence and Democracy*, 278.

38. Jacqueline Rose, *On Not Being Able to Sleep at Night* (Princeton: Princeton University Press, 2003), 217.

39. Mahmood Mamdani talks about this in terms of "willed versus structural outcomes." See Mamdani, "Beyond Nuremberg," in Engle, Miller, and Davis, *Anti-Impunity*, 345. See also Richard Wilson, *The Politics of Truth and Reconciliation in South Africa: Legitimizing the Post-Apartheid State* (Cambridge: Cambridge University Press, 2001), 93.

40. Robert Meister, *After Evil: A Politics of Human Rights* (New York: Columbia University Press, 2011), 24.

41. Meister, 28.

42. "The TRC, by looking to the wisdom of international precepts as a guide to its conclusions, will bolster its own domestic authority along with the authority of those global precepts that were a feature of the country's deliverance from what went before." Asmal, Asmal, and Roberts, *Reconciliation Through Truth*, 205.

43. Samera Esmeir, *Juridical Humanity: A Colonial History* (Stanford: Stanford University Press, 2012), 11.

44. Tutu, *No Future Without Forgiveness*, 106.

45. Tutu, 107. On the determination of the ANC's failure to use "just means," see Truth and Reconciliation Commission Report, 2:325.

46. Asmal, Asmal, and Roberts, *Reconciliation Through Truth*, 114.

47. Asmal, Asmal, and Roberts, 121.

48. Asmal, Asmal, and Roberts, 214.

49. Truth and Reconciliation Commission Report, 5:347.

50. Richard Wilson, "Reconciliation and Revenge in Post-Apartheid South Africa," *Current Anthropology* 41, no. 1 (2000): 80.

51. Cited in Sitze, *The Impossible Machine*, 39.

52. Sitze, 84.

53. Sitze, 125–26.

54. Sitze, 126.

55. Sitze, 127.

56. Truth and Reconciliation Commission Report, 5:309.

57. Asmal, Asmal, and Roberts, *Reconciliation Through Truth*, 141.

58. Truth and Reconciliation Commission Report, 5:319.

59. David Johnson, "Theorizing the Loss of Land: Griqua Land Claims in Southern Africa," in *Loss: The Politics of Mourning*, ed. David Eng and David Kazanjian (Berkeley: University of California Press, 2003), 290.

60. Mamdani, "Beyond Nuremberg," 339.

61. Truth and Reconciliation Commission Report, 5:308.

62. Truth and Reconciliation Commission Report, 5:349.

63. Wilson, *The Politics of Truth*, 97.

64. Karl Marx, "On the Jewish Question," in *The Marx-Engels Reader*, ed. Robert Tucker (New York: Norton, 1978), 33.

65. Wilson, *The Politics of Truth*, 93.

66. Tutu, *No Future Without Forgiveness*, 273.

67. Asmal, Asmal, and Roberts, *Reconciliation Through Truth*, 214.

68. Asmal, Asmal, and Roberts, 9.

69. Tutu, *No Future Without Forgiveness*, 265.

70. Truth and Reconciliation Commission Report, 1:134.
71. Truth and Reconciliation Commission Report, 1:48.
72. Michel de Certeau, *The Practice of Everyday Life*, trans. Steven Rendall (Berkeley: University of California Press, 1984), 128.

3. Calling History to Account

1. The best history of these demands is Ana Lucia Araujo, *Reparations for Slavery and the Slave Trade: A Transnational and Comparative History* (London: Bloomsbury, 2017).
2. Araujo, 91.
3. Sven Beckert and Seth Rockman, eds., *Slavery's Capitalism: A New History of American Economic Development* (Philadelphia: University of Pennsylvania Press, 2016), 3.
4. Ta-Nehisi Coates, *We Were Eight Years in Power: An American Tragedy* (New York: One World, 2017), 347.
5. Stephen Best and Saidya Hartman, "Fugitive Justice," *Representations* 92 (Fall 2005): 1–2.
6. Beginning in 1952, Germany paid compensation to Holocaust victims. The TRC recommended $360 million for the nineteen thousand victims who had testified before the Commission. It was not until 2003 that a one-time payment of about $3900 was offered by government of Thabo Mbeki, much to the distress of the victims who thought it was too little too late. Ginger Thompson, "South Africa to Pay $3900 to Each Family of Apartheid Victims," *New York Times*, April 16, 2003, www.nytimes.com /2003/04/16/world/south-africa-to-pay-3900-to-each-family -of-apartheid-victims.html.
7. Aaron Carico, "Freedom as Accumulation," *History of the Present 6*, no. 1 (2016): 24–25.
8. David Scott, "Preface: A Reparatory History of the Present," *Small Axe* 52 (March 2017): x.
9. David Scott, "Evil Beyond Repair," *Small Axe* 55 (March 2018): x.
10. Coates, *Eight Years*, 158.

11. US Senate, "Landmark Legislation: Thirteenth, Fourteenth, and Fifteenth Amendments," www.senate.gov/artandhistory/history/common/generic/CivilWarAmendments.htm.

12. At the beginning of 1867, no African American in the South held political office, but within three or four years about 15 percent of the officeholders in the South were black. On the history of Reconstruction, see W. E. B. Du Bois, *Black Reconstruction in America, 1860–1880* (New York: Free, 1998); and Eric Foner, *Reconstruction: America's Unfinished Revolution* (New York: Harper, 2014).

13. Carico, "Freedom as Accumulation," 1.

14. Carico, 4.

15. Carico, 6.

16. Carico, 23–24.

17. Carico, 11.

18. Indeed, after passage of the act in 1935, 65 percent of African Americans nationally and 70 percent to 80 percent of them in the South were ineligible for support, leading an NAACP spokesman to describe this new American safety net as "a sieve with holes just big enough for the majority of Negroes to fall through." Coates, *Eight Years*, 186.

19. In Chicago, for example, the Federal Housing Authority (FHA) openly endorsed segregated housing, leading one commentator to note that "the FHA adopted a racial policy that could well have been called for in the Nuremberg laws." Coates, *Eight Years*, 169. The area of housing was a particularly stark example of racial exclusion; from government-backed loan agencies (which adhered to restrictive covenants for sales and rentals) to local enforcement that protected white privilege, housing markets maintained not only geographic segregation but all that went with it, including segregated schools.

20. History.com, "Brown v. Board of Education Ruling," www.history.com/topics/black-history/brown-v-board-of-education-of-topeka. In the wake of *Brown*, schools in the South were integrated, even as many white parents enrolled their children in private (typically Christian) academies. Black teachers and principals

were often demoted or lost their jobs entirely since white teachers were given priority in newly integrated schools.

21. "Memorandum by Mr. Justice Jackson," unpublished, 2. See David O'Brien, "Justice R. H. Jackson's Unpublished Opinion in Brown v. Board of Education," *SCOTUSblog*. I am grateful to Robert Post for this reference.

22. "Memorandum by Mr. Justice Jackson," 1. Jackson succumbed to the pressure for a unanimous decision. This may have had to do with Cold War imperatives: the USSR was using racial injustice in the United States as an indictment of capitalist democracy.

23. Coates, *Eight Years*, 334.

24. Despite dogged resistance from those (especially in the South) who sought to undermine the laws if they could, both acts opened a period of heightened expectation and significant change. More African Americans voted and won office, even in the South, where federal oversight of states with long records of voter suppression led to important reform. In reaction, racial gerrymandering of electoral districts intensified and party realignments (the Democrats became the face of liberal policies, the Republicans of white conservatism) sharpened political divides based on race.

25. Some critics argue that when affirmative action is redefined in terms of "diversity," it takes the inclusion of blacks (and other minorities) to be not so much for their benefit—as a form of reparation or compensation—as for the benefit of white majorities who will become more accepting of "others" when exposed to them.

26. John David Skrentny, *The Ironies of Affirmative Action: Politics, Culture, and Justice in America* (Chicago: University of Chicago Press, 1996).

27. Angela Hanks, Danyelle Solomon, and Christian E. Weller, "Systematic Inequality: How America's Structural Racism Helped Create the Black-White Wealth Gap," Center for American Progress website, www.americanprogress.org/issues/race/reports/2018/02/21/447051/systematic-inequality/3.

28. Hanks, Solomon, and Weller, 3.

29. Hanks, Solomon, and Weller, 19.

30. Blacks are 12 percent of the US population and 33 percent of the prison population. A study in 2003 of the effects of felony convictions on job applicants "showed that blacks who said they had a criminal record had a callback rate of 5 percent, and blacks who said they did not had a rate of 14 percent. For whites, the rates were 17 percent . . . and 34 percent." Deborah Pager, *Marked: Race, Crime, and Finding Work in an Era of Mass Incarceration* (Chicago: University of Chicago Press, 2008). The citation appears in her obituary in the *New York Times*, November 9, 2018.

31. Hanks, Solomon, and Weller, "Systematic Inequality," 34.

32. Randall Robinson, *The Debt: What America Owes to Blacks* (New York: Plume, 2001), 107.

33. Martha Biondi, "The Rise of the Reparations Movement," *Radical History Review* 87 (Fall 2003): 9.

34. Stefano Harney and Fred Moten, *The Undercommons: Fugitive Planning and Black Study*, www.minorcompositions.info/wp-content/uploads/2013/04/undercommons-web.pdf.

35. In 1848, Walker's pamphlet was republished by Henry Highland Garnet with a more explicit call for slaves to demand wages or go on strike (using violence if they had to). David Walker and Henry Highland Garnet, *Walker's Appeal, with a Brief Sketch of His Life by Henry Highland Garnet and Also Garnet's Address to the Slaves of the United States of America* (New York: J. H. Tobitt, 1848). Thanks to Andrew Zimmerman for this reference.

36. Araujo, *Reparations for Slavery*, 42, 52.

37. Araujo, 104.

38. Araujo, 94.

39. Araujo, 142.

40. Araujo, 140.

41. James Forman, "Black Manifesto," *New York Review of Books*, July 10, 1969.

42. Robinson, *The Debt*, 107.

43. Robinson, 207.

44. David Scott, "Preface: Debt, Redress," *Small Axe* 18, no. 1 (2014): ix.

45. See Alondra Nelson, *The Social Life of DNA: Race, Reparation, and Knowledge After the Genome* (Boston: Beacon, 2016), chap. 4, for a discussion of the ways DNA has been used to fortify reparations claims.

46. Forman did not rule out armed struggle in the United States either. In his *Manifesto* peaceful demands for a Southern land bank, black publishing houses, black TV networks, and skill-training centers as well as a Black Anti-Defamation League sat alongside declarations of war, in the form of calls for disruptions of church services, sit-ins, and other unspecified means of self-defense and national liberation.

47. Robinson, *The Debt*, 17.

48. Robinson, 218–20.

49. Robinson, 216.

50. Coates, *Eight Years*, 288.

51. Coates, xiii.

52. US Congress, HR 40, Commission to Study and Develop Reparation Proposals for African-Americans Act, 115th Congress (2017–18), www.congress.gov/bill/115th-congress/house-bill/40.

53. Coates, *Eight Years*, 37.

54. Coates, 43.

55. Coates, 138.

56. Coates, 68.

57. Coates, 80.

58. Coates, 69 (my emphasis).

59. See Sarah Juliet Lauro, *The Transatlantic Zombie: Slavery, Rebellion and Living Death* (New Brunswick, NJ: Rutgers University Press, 2015), especially "Introduction: Zombie Dialectics—'Ki Sa Sa Ye?' (What Is That?)," 4.

60. Lauro, 4.

61. Here I want to disagree with Adolph Reed's dismissal of Coates's arguments as suggesting that racism is "an intractable, transhistorical force. . . . [that] lies beyond structural intervention." In contrast, I read Coates not as an "exhortation to individual

conversion and repentance as a program," but as a call for collective political action—for the kind of blasting open of conventional history that Walter Benjamin called for. Adolph Reed, "The Trouble with Uplift," *Baffler*, September 2018, https://thebaffler.com/salvos/the-trouble-with-uplift-reed.

62. Sigmund Freud, "Mourning and Melancholia," in *The Standard Edition of the Complete Psychological Works of Sigmund Freud*, trans. James Strachey (London: Hogarth, 1995), 14:243.

63. Coates, *Eight Years*, 109, 66.

64. Coates, 64.

65. Coates, 159.

66. Coates, 104.

67. Coates, 112.

68. Coates, 367.

69. Coates, 159.

70. David L. Eng and David Kazanjian, eds., *Loss: The Politics of Mourning* (Berkeley: University of California Press, 2003), 4.

71. Dana Luciano, "Passing Shadows: Melancholic Nationality and Black Critical Publicity in Pauline E. Hopkins *Of One Blood*," in Eng and Kazanjian, *Loss*, 149.

72. Robinson, *The Debt*, 220.

73. Robinson, 232.

74. Robinson, 243.

75. Robinson, 149.

76. Coates, *Eight Years*, 202.

77. Coates, 180.

78. Scott, "Preface: Debt, Redress," x.

79. "The 1619 Project," *New York Times Magazine*, August 14, 2019, 5.

Epilogue

1. Human Rights Watch, "South Africa: Attacks on Foreign Nationals," April 15, 2019, www.hrw.org/news/2019/04/15/south-africa-attacks-foreign-nationals#.

2. Wendy Brown, *States of Injury: Power and Freedom in Late Modernity* (Princeton: Princeton University Press, 1995), 74.

3. Brown, 71.

4. Brown, 76.

5. Jacques Derrida, *Specters of Marx: The State of the Debt, the Work of Mourning, and the New International*, trans. Peggy Kamuf (New York: Routledge, 1994), 59.

6. Derrida, 75.

7. Fredric Jameson, "The Politics of Utopia," *New Left Review* 25 (2004).

8. Gary Wilder, "Anticipation," *Political Concepts*, 5. https://www.political concepts.org/anticipation-gary-wilder/. See also Massimiliano Tomba, "Justice and Divine Violence: Walter Benjamin and the Time of Anticipation," *Theory and Event* 20, no. 3 (2017): 579–98.

9. Mark Fisher, *Capitalist Realism: Is There No Alternative?* (United Kingdom: Zero, 2009), 79.

10. Michael Löwy, *Fire Alarm: Reading Walter Benjamin's "On the Concept of History,"* trans. Chris Turner (London: Verso, 2016), 105.

11. Michel Foucault, "What Is Critique?," in *The Politics of Truth: Michel Foucault*, ed. Sylvére Lotringer and Lysa Hochroch (New York: Semiotext[e], 1997), 44.

12. Foucault, 46.

13. Ta-Nehisi Coates, *We Were Eight Years in Power: An American Tragedy* (New York: One World, 2017), chap. 4, "The Legacy of Malcolm X."

14. Massimiliano Tomba, "Sanctuaries as Anachronism and Anticipation," *History of the Present* 9, no. 2 (2019): 222. See also Tomba, *Insurgent Universality: An Alternative Legacy of Modernity* (New York: Oxford University Press, 2019).

15. Tomba, "Sanctuaries," 223.

16. Tomba, 219.

17. Walter Benjamin, "Central Park," cited in Löwy, *Fire Alarm*, 84.

INDEX

Hopkins, Pauline, 74
Horkheimer, Max, xii
human rights: Israel and, 19;
justice associated with, 16;
national sovereignty in
conflict with, xx, 7, 19;
nation-states as protectors of,
19, 21; in Nuremberg trials, 4,
7, 16, 21; in South Africa,
33–34, 40, 42–44; universalist
premise of, xviii, xx

identity politics, 83
imperialism, xix–xx, 10, 12,
13–14
Inkatha Freedom Party (IFP),
24
International Labor
Organization, 37
international law: apartheid as
violation of, 37; imperialism
not restrained by, 14; and
nation-state sovereignty, xx;
in Nuremberg context, 2–4;
protective function of, 19; and
warfare, 11
International Military Tribunal,
Nuremberg, Germany. See
Nuremberg trials
Israel, 19–20, 96n56

Jackson, Robert, xxi, 1, 3–7,
9–13, 15–17, 59–60, 94n15,
103n22
Jameson, Fredric, 83

Jews: and founding of Israel,
19–20; genocidal plans
against, 5, 9–10, 20;
international intervention on
behalf of, 7, 10
Johnson, Andrew, 56
Judgment at Nuremberg (film), 14
judgment of history: appeals to
moral authority of, ix–xv,
79–80, 82, 87; finality
imputed to, 79–80;
Nuremberg trials and, 1–3,
16, 21, 80; refusals of, ix–x,
35; slavery reparations and,
52, 74, 76; the state's
enactment of, xviii, xx–xxi,
xxii–xxiii, 6, 18, 21, 81; TRC
and, 23, 25, 27, 48, 50; truth
to be revealed by, xii, 79; uses
of the concept of, xiii, 76–77
justice: alternative standards of,
86; forgiveness in relation to,
26–27, 30; in Nuremberg
trials, 1–3, 5–6, 21; slavery
reparations and, 53, 54, 74; in
South Africa, 37–38; the
state identified with, xviii, 6,
80, 87; in TRC context,
23–27, 33

Kant, Immanuel, xv
Kellogg-Briand pact, 11
King, Martin Luther, xi, 65, 73
Koselleck, Reinhart, xiv–xvi
Ku Klux Klan, ix, 57, 79